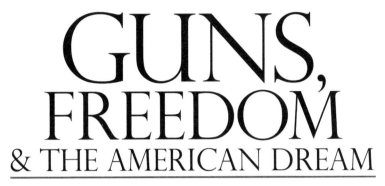

GUNS, FREEDOM
& THE AMERICAN DREAM

The Story of Tim Schmidt and the USCCA

Published By:
Delta Defense, LLC
West Bend, WI, USA

www.GunsFreedomAmericanDream.com

Delta Defense, LLC
300 South 6th Avenue
West Bend, WI 53095
www.DeltaDefense.com

Printed in the United States of America
10 9 8 7 6 5 4 3 2 1

Library of Congress Cataloging-In-Publication Data:
Schmidt, Tim
Guns, Freedom & The American Dream: The Story of
Tim Schmidt and the USCCA / Tim Schmidt

ISBN 978-0-9967874-0-6 (hard cover)

1. Biography 2. Entrepreneur 3. Firearms 4. Politics

First edition.

Editing by Laurie Arendt
Editing by Carla Dickmann
Proofreading by Laura Otto
Cover Photo by Ken Wangler
Author Photo by Jessica Burns
Cover Design by Noelle McPike
Book Layout by Kelly Welke

Distributed by Delta Defense, LLC
www.DeltaDefense.com

Significant discounts for bulk sales are available. Please contact Delta Defense, LLC | USCCA, Inc. at 877-677-1919.

This book is dedicated to my wife, Tonnie, who has stuck by me through untold trials and tribulations. She believed in me when she probably shouldn't have. This book is also dedicated to Tim Jr., Dagny, and Sten, my three amazing children. I am so proud of the young adults you've turned into. It is an honor to be your father, protector, and defender!

ACKNOWLEDGEMENTS

I have so many people I need to thank. I'll start with my father. Dad, thank you for teaching me discipline, work ethic, and perseverance. The words "If it is to be, it's up to me" will always ring in my head thanks to you. Your support and belief in me have given me strength in dark hours that I've never shared with you. Next is my mother. Mom, thank you for teaching me unending optimism, gentleness, and unconditional love. I realize it's almost a cliché to tell your Mom that she's a saint, but Mom, "You're a saint!" I feel so blessed and fortunate to have been raised by two parents who lead with love, discipline, and kindness. Thank you both!

Thanks to the entire Delta Defense family. I appreciate each and every one of you. We're on a mission together and I know that you guys have my back.

GUNS, FREEDOM &
THE AMERICAN DREAM

"Tim Schmidt's story truly embodies the American Dream. He found something he believed in, worked to become an expert in his field, and built an amazing business around what he loved. Prior to coming to the USCCA, I worked in the firearms industry for nearly two decades—and in all that time, I never felt the power of commitment like Tim brings to an organization. His energy and commitment should serve as an inspiration to every American."

- **Kevin Michalowski**
  Executive Editor, *Concealed Carry Magazine*

"I had the honor of meeting Tim Schmidt when the USCCA was but a one-man operation, a fledgling magazine, and a giant dream. Since that day years ago, that man and his dream have profoundly changed my life. More importantly, I have watched his dream grow to touch the lives of millions of others. I know Tim as a man of incredible integrity and high moral character; a man of faith and family. Through the words on these pages, his dreams will also touch you and inspire you to reach for yours."

- **Mark Walters**
  Nationally Syndicated Radio Talk Show Host,
  Armed American Radio

"This is one of the most important books of our time. This is a story that gives important insight into the dominant political movement of our generation. This is the history of the incredible rise of the USCCA: a great organization, and a powerful innovative force for good in our nation. And this is a shining example of the difference that one man can make in a free nation.

Every gun owner should read this book. Everyone who cares about our God-given gun rights and the ongoing, never-ending battle to protect our freedom and the American way of life should own this book. Everyone who is willing to stand up for the American Dream—and everyone who would learn about the "fundamentally silly" arguments (yes, that is what he calls them!) of the insidious individuals who would attack and undermine our way of life— should read and learn from this book.

Thomas Jefferson told us that 'eternal vigilance is the price of liberty,' and two centuries later, Tim Schmidt is the living personification of that eternal vigilance (and of the Constitutional right and social obligation to carry a gun). Tim is a true American entrepreneur who walked the road less traveled. He is the man in the arena who took great risks, dared greatly, and achieved the laurel of victory and fame.

Tim is a personal hero of mine, he is a man I am honored to call a friend, and he is a truly great American who will inform and inspire you."

- **Lt. Col. Dave Grossman, U.S. Army (Ret.)**
  Author, *On Combat* and *On Killing*
  Co-author, *Control: Exposing the Truth About Guns*
  (with Glenn Beck)

"This book is about more than just the importance of gun rights. It's more than a book about the birth of the United States Concealed Carry Association or Concealed Carry Magazine.

It's a story about the entrepreneurial spirit—about a man who had a vision and who refused to let that vision die, even when confronted by the overwhelming struggles of trying to start something from scratch.

It's a story about passion. It's a story about failures and successes.

But ultimately, it's a story about Tim Schmidt: a man who truly understands the importance of freedom and who will never stop fighting for it. I'm incredibly proud to call him my friend."

- **Sheriff David A. Clarke, Jr.**
  Milwaukee County, Wisconsin

"Tim Schmidt's new book applies advanced marketing and entre-preneurship principles to the fight for gun owners' civil rights."

- **Massad Ayoob**
  Author, *In the Gravest Extreme* and *Deadly Force: Understanding Your Right to Self-Defense*

CONTENTS

A MESSAGE FROM THE PEOPLE'S SHERIFF

When I first met Tim Schmidt in the summer of 2013, I was in the middle of garnering national attention for a public service announcement I had released earlier that year. In that PSA, I reminded citizens of Milwaukee County (Wisconsin) that *they* are the first line of defense in their own personal safety. Up until that point, I had spent the majority of my 35 years in law enforcement—11 as sheriff of Milwaukee County—as a relative unknown outside Milwaukee.

But when I truthfully said that calling 911 and waiting for help was no longer the best option for residents of the city I swore to serve and protect, the left-wing media, not surprisingly, took quick notice. When I urged the good men and women in my community to consider taking a certified firearms safety course so they could righteously fight back against violent criminals, I was excoriated in the press as a "gun-crazy" sheriff. And when I unapologetically suggested that it was the *duty of all Americans* to protect themselves and their families, I went from being a locally known sheriff to a nationally recognized enemy of the anti-gun crowd almost overnight.

In hindsight, releasing that PSA was a common sense move, but apparently not to statists who think you should outsource your personal security to the government. Although the ideas I expressed in that message weren't revolutionary to *me*—I had always felt that people play a role in their personal safety—I imagine it came as

1

quite a shock to some people to hear the sheriff of Wisconsin's most populous county admit that the government isn't necessarily the best first option when the "fit hits the shan" as the country music song says.

The PSA had positive *and* negative implications for me on both personal and professional levels. On one hand, I had to deal with the constant onslaught of negative publicity. On the other hand, the PSA lent a much needed voice to the pro-gun crowd. It expressed what many people were thinking and feeling but were afraid to say out loud. It brought the importance of citizens accepting responsibility for their own safety into the national spotlight. It launched me as an ally—a leader, even—of responsibly armed Americans all across the country...and honestly, what an honor that has been.

That PSA is also what prompted Tim to reach out to me in July 2013. To be honest, I had never heard of him or the USCCA, but I did a little research and was impressed by what I found. I arranged for a face-to-face meeting at my office in downtown Milwaukee, and it didn't take long for me to realize we had a few very important things in common. Tim *and* his organization were in perfect alignment with my beliefs about the Second Amendment and personal defense. I remember thinking to myself, "Wow. Here is someone who really 'gets it.'" See, when it comes to gun rights, self-defense, and personal responsibility, there really isn't a middle ground. And Tim Schmidt and I were very clearly on the same side of the fence.

I actually reached out to Tim later that fall after exchanging occasional private emails. As it turned out, the Milwaukee County Board of Supervisors was attempting to muzzle my PSA by making it illegal for an elected official to appear in such an announcement. I asked Tim for help, and he responded by reaching out to the USCCA community, asking them to stand against this injustice. Soon the phone lines at the Milwaukee County Board of Supervisors were clogged with polite but passionate disagreement with their attempt to keep me quiet. It worked. They blinked and pulled the resolution back.

Around this time, Tim and the rest of the USCCA crew moved into their new headquarters in West Bend, Wisconsin. Tim reached out to me in late 2013—the same year I was, much to my surprise and much to the chagrin of the anti-gunners, named Sheriff of the Year—and asked if I'd be willing to speak at an open house event he was planning for February of the following year. I was honored, and quickly agreed.

Our relationship would become especially important in the months leading up to my re-election in 2014, which was becoming something of a national issue thanks, in part, to that controversial PSA and the ensuing media attention. I found myself in some political hot water; the Left was out to get me. Mayor Michael Bloomberg made it a personal goal to remove me as Milwaukee County Sheriff.

I had no intention of letting that happen, but it was clear I needed some help. And so I turned once again to Tim and asked him if there was anything he could do. His response?

"Sheriff Clarke, give me a week and I'll start making things happen."

Well, Tim's words were NOT an empty promise. As I quickly found out, Tim's audience over at the USCCA was loyal *and* willing to take action, just as they had proved when they inundated the Milwaukee County Board with their phone calls. Tim sent a short series of emails to his almost 2 million subscribers and soon donations to my re-election campaign began pouring in. It was the extra boost of support I needed, and I look back on his gesture with extreme gratitude.

It turns out that Tim Schmidt is NOT just a man who shares my belief in the natural-born right to self-defense; he is also a man of his word, one who is willing to do whatever it takes to fight the good fight for the responsibly armed citizen.

I've continued to learn more and more about Tim and his organization and what they've done for the cause.

Some (especially) impressive things:

- The USCCA's Amicus Brief in the landmark *McDonald vs. Chicago* U.S. Supreme Court Case was one of only two briefs that was cited by Justice Alito in the "winning decision."

- Tim was named in the top 100 most influential gun rights activists by *Newsmax.*

- The USCCA hosted a Concealed Carry Expo in 2015, a first-of-its-kind event at which I had the privilege to speak.

And most importantly:

- The USCCA has saved countless responsibly armed Americans from unmeritorious persecution and possible jail time after life-saving self-defense incidents.

Tim has, quite literally, built an empire of gun-loving patriots who are willing to stand up for what's right.

But this book is about more than just the importance of gun rights. It's more than a book about the birth of the United States Concealed Carry Association or *Concealed Carry Magazine*.

It's a story about the entrepreneurial spirit—about a man who had a vision and who *refused* to let that vision die, even when confronted by the overwhelming struggles of trying to start something from scratch.

It's a story about passion. It's a story about failures and successes.

But ultimately, it's a story about Tim Schmidt: a man who truly understands the importance of freedom and who will never stop fighting for it. I'm incredibly proud to call him my friend.

- Sheriff David A. Clarke, Jr.

CHAPTER 1

FULL CIRCLE

> *I joined the USCCA because my wife (of 46 years), our three grown children, and our 11 grandchildren deserve all of the protection I can provide. Unfortunately it isn't 1955 anymore.*
>
> *– William B., TN*

In late April of 2014, I experienced one of those rare moments in life when certain things finally seem to come full circle.

Let me explain.

I was heading home from the annual NRA Meeting & Exhibits in Indianapolis, Indiana, and as I sat there on the plane, a bit of nostalgia set in. I couldn't help but think of how much had changed over the last decade or so. You see, it was on a notorious flight some 15 years earlier that I had first read Robert Boatman's "The Constitutional Right and Social Obligation to Carry a Gun"—an article that awoke my inner patriot and—quite honestly—changed my *entire* life.

That article inspired me, as a new father, to take responsibility for my family's safety. To do whatever it takes to protect the ones I love. I guess you could even say that it inspired me to do *exactly* what I'm doing today: helping responsibly armed Americans across the country be the best protectors they can be. You see, that article is where *Concealed Carry Magazine* first found its roots. And the guiding principles in that article provided the foundation on which I built the United States Concealed Carry Association.

Of course, things weren't always easy. In fact, creating a gun magazine and a national firearms association wasn't always on my radar.

The early "plan" was pretty straightforward: I wanted to be an engineer. And as a relatively shy, self-proclaimed "geek," that path made perfect sense.

After high school, I headed off to Michigan Technological University, and I absolutely LOVED it there. Back then, 85% of all students at Michigan Tech were studying to be engineers, and that meant I was *finally* in my element. (Well, at least I didn't feel like a complete geek anymore...because EVERYONE was a geek!) It was great, and as far as I was concerned, it was the perfect fit for me. And things worked out mostly according to plan: 5 years later, I had a Bachelor's Degree in Mechanical Engineering and a beautiful new wife, Tonnie, who I met and married during my time there.

Shortly after graduation, Tonnie and I moved out to Boston (where she had managed to snag a really cool job working on the "Big Dig"). We lived in a crappy little apartment in a nearby town called Natick (about 18 miles from downtown). I remember Tonnie riding her bike to and from work every day.

In the meantime, I had finally managed to get a job as a mechanical engineer at IEC, a company that made medical equipment. Despite my inexperience (maybe you know the feeling: starting out someplace new and realizing how *little* you know about everything), I enjoyed what I was doing and got to design some pretty cool stuff. I quickly learned that having the title of "engineer" meant that people listened to what I had to say, despite the fact that I was still the "new guy." I also learned that despite being (mostly) interested and engaged in what I was doing, there was a large part of me that was already feeling restless (and honestly, this is a trend you'll probably pick up on throughout this book). I just couldn't shake the feeling of wanting something *more*.

So when Shawn, a pushy guy from a company called New Technology Solutions, came to IEC to sell us some "high-end" computer workstations for the new engineering software we were starting to use, offered to buy me lunch, and asked me if I'd like to double my salary, I was already primed to say "yes."

"Just tell me what I have to do," I told him.

Shawn wanted me to help him sell his high-end computer workstations. And since I was an engineer and most of his prospects were also engineers, he figured that I'd be the perfect guy for the job. (In reality, this was his "nice" way of telling me he thought I could "geek-talk" other engineers into buying his product!) With thoughts of making more money, I quickly agreed.

When I look back on that decision, it doesn't necessarily make a whole lot of sense. I mean, there I was, a guy who had just spent five years of his life getting a degree in engineering, accepting a job *selling computers!* Honestly, it was a risky (crazy?) move at the time, but I never doubted it. And now that my life has unfolded in a completely different way than I expected, I look back to that moment as one that taught me to trust myself and my instincts. I guess I've always refused to "settle" when there are so many opportunities just waiting for me to make a move.

As it turns out, selling computers came easy to me. Even though I wasn't much of a "people person," I found it wasn't a big deal to talk to prospects on the phone. Without the pressure of face-to-face meetings—and with the confidence that I really knew my stuff—I became a lot more outgoing.

I quickly learned that I could become a different person when talking to someone on the phone. (I realize now that this was an early lesson in sales and marketing but also in human psychology—something I've studied in depth over the years and that ultimately plays an integral role in what I do today.) I learned that perception is everything; if you can deliver what your customer wants, it doesn't matter if your office doubles as your living room and your desk is a T.V. tray. You CAN and SHOULD go up against the goliaths in your industry. You'd be amazed at how easy it is to compete against them when you can deliver the right product to the right people at the right time.

The other big thing I learned working with Shawn was the importance of rapid execution. Shawn was an insecure guy who wasn't really that smart, yet he had built this incredibly profitable and rapidly growing business from scratch. I thought to myself, "Heck, if *this* guy can start and run a successful business, then I sure as heck can, too." See, the ONE thing that gave Shawn his massive success was that he *always* took massive action. He was no genius, but he never sat around making excuses. I never did care for Shawn much, but there's no denying I learned a *lot* from that guy. In fact, working for Shawn gave me the courage to start my own engineering business.

After about a year of selling computers for Shawn, Tonnie and I decided it was time to return to Wisconsin. Since we were both in need of new jobs and since I wanted to get back into engineering, we decided it would be the perfect time to give our own engineering consulting business a go. It didn't matter much to either of us that I had less than a year's experience under my belt.

There was just something about being able to say, "Yep, we own our own business" that appealed to us both.

You'll hear the full story later in the book, but we launched Schmidt Engineering, Inc. (SEI) out of our apartment in Muskego, Wisconsin on July 8th, 1997. I didn't really know what I was doing on *many* levels, but I was *very* determined...and I took action.

To say that SEI was a struggle would be a *huge* understatement. It was actually a gigantic struggle. I can't even remember how long it took to turn a profit (I've developed an uncanny ability to selectively repress bad memories).

But Tonnie and I persevered. We worked many, many long hours to develop relationships with customers who would in turn recommend our little engineering firm to other companies. We limped along from little victory to roadblock and back again for many months. I sometimes refer to this time as "feast or famine." We were either making a lot of money or absolutely nothing at all.

Within a couple of years, things slowly took off and we were able to move Schmidt Engineering out of our apartment and into a real office. We were even able to hire our first employee. Our reputation as a solid engineering firm was also starting to take hold in the marketplace, and suddenly we had a half-dozen engineers on staff. But as the business grew, so did the headaches. The money was good, but I was tired and restless. Honestly, there were so many ups and downs...and I just wasn't sure how much longer I could stay on the roller coaster.

When we found out that Tonnie was pregnant, I began to seriously consider other options. The engineering business was running smoothly, but my heart just wasn't in it.

What my heart *was* in was this notion of becoming a father. And when Tim Jr. was born, I just felt *different.* Suddenly, I had this brand new baby who was dependent on me for absolutely *everything.* (If you're a parent, you know what I'm talking about.) It was incredible and exciting and scary all at once, and it ignited in me an unwavering desire to do everything in my power to keep him safe. I guess that's why Robert Boatman's article hit me so hard.

I knew I had to do *something.*

As it turns out, that "something" meant learning *anything* and *everything* I could about firearms and self-defense.

There was only one (legitimate) problem: there simply wasn't enough information out there to help me get started. There weren't any books or magazines dedicated to the concealed carry lifestyle, and there were no resources available to help me feel confident in protecting myself and my family with a gun. Heck, even a trip to my local gun shop left me frustrated and downright angry (you'll hear *that* whole story a little later).

But here's the thing: I'm what some people call a "doer." I like to get stuff done. So when I'm on a "mission," there is almost nothing that can stop me. And when you factor in something as important as my family's safety...well, let's just say I was *extra* driven at that point.

Now, if you're already familiar with the USCCA, you probably know what happened next:

I decided to start a magazine.

Yep, since I couldn't find the information I wanted from outside sources, I decided to create it myself. I mean, I couldn't possibly be the only guy out there who was looking to protect his family.

Did I have any magazine publishing experience? No. Did I have a partner who knew what they were doing? No. So what in the heck was I thinking when I decided to start a magazine from ground zero? Quite honestly, I jumped in *without* really thinking. But a few key decisions saved me from a potentially disastrous result.

First off, I selected an excellent market. (I simply cannot over-emphasize how important this is. Proper market selection is the grease that will make almost every other aspect of your business run smoothly.) I also studied successful people in the industry. (Ever been told not to reinvent the wheel? Well, turns out this is legit advice. I copied proven marketing promotions to launch my business.)

During the initial hard times—and there were a *lot* of hard times— I focused 100% on learning to be a world-class marketer. And most importantly, *I never quit.*

Back in January of 2004—when I had finally produced the very first physical issue of *Concealed Carry Magazine*—a small part of me thought I had really "hit it big." The 30,000 "sample" copies I had sent out with a subscription offer had yielded about 1,000 customers...and that meant I *had* to keep moving forward. (This turned out to be both a blessing and a curse, as you'll find out a little later.) In that moment, despite having spent countless hours producing that first issue and completely exhausting my and Tonnie's bank account, I remember feeling so proud and so confident.

I was so confident, in fact, that shortly after that first issue was printed, I was headed down to my first ever SHOT Show in Las Vegas, armed with *hundreds* of copies. I had even invited my dad along to help me pass them out. I was over-the-moon excited. You see, I was convinced that *everyone* would be lining up to get their hands on *Concealed Carry Magazine.*

Boy, was I ever wrong. People had no clue who I was or what I did, and not a single person showed any interest in my magazine. It's hard to admit this, but that was one of the lowest, most embarrassing moments of my entire life.

I knew I *believed* in what I was doing. I also felt in my heart it was what I was *supposed* to be doing. So what was the problem?

I started to fear that maybe I had jumped the gun a bit.

You see, I had made the mistake of thinking I had "made it." I made the mistake of believing that after one small success, the work was somehow done. I made the mistake of focusing on what I had already accomplished (produced a magazine) instead of what I was trying to do (educate responsibly armed Americans).

The truth is, I had been fighting so hard and for so long that I was desperate for a win. Somewhere along the way, I had lost focus. I had lost my momentum.

Needless to say, I knew that something had to change.

There's a Winston Churchill quote I've always loved that I think hits the nail on the head here. He said, "Success is not final, failure is not fatal: it is the courage to continue that counts."

And so back in 2004, I left my first ever SHOT Show with nearly every single copy of *Concealed Carry Magazine* I had come with. But with my dad by my side, I felt a renewed sense of responsibility to prove that this experience was only a small bump in the road. I *needed* to find a way to make it work. I *needed* to find a way to make him proud, to draw strength from the words he had shared so long ago and which had inspired me ever since: "If it is to be, it's up to me." (You'll hear a *lot* about this a little later.)

Luckily, things *did* take a turn for the better.

I still can't remember how I stumbled upon his website, but sometime toward the end of 2005, I bought a fitness product over the internet from a guy named Matt Furey. It was called "Combat Conditioning."

The product itself was a booklet and a DVD. It was a great product that taught body-weight exercises. I read the booklet and watched the DVD...and then a few weeks later, I received a letter from this Matt Furey guy. He was offering to sell me a CD package called "Magnetic Millionaire." I bought the package and listened to the CDs as soon as they arrived. They were fantastic. They reminded me of the books and tapes that my dad made me listen to when I was a teenager (more on that later).

A few weeks after that I received *another* letter from Matt. This time he was selling a product called "Magnetic Marketing." It was a no brainer. I ordered it right away.

When that package arrived, I realized that Matt Furey was actually *reselling* all of these products for the guy who actually produced them. And *that* guy's name was Dan Kennedy.

I did a search for Dan Kennedy on the internet and was inundated with a tremendous amount of information. Turns out he was pretty well known in the marketing world. I promptly subscribed to his monthly newsletter and opened myself up to as much direct marketing information as I could handle.

Somewhere in this phase of exhaustive internet research, I stumbled upon a Yanik Silver website. If you're not familiar with Yanik Silver, he's an entrepreneur, author, and digital marketing expert. Anyway, he was selling these special "top secret" silver briefcases that had the DVDs, CDs, and workbooks from his very first "Underground Online Marketing" Seminar. Well, he only had a limited number of these briefcases available, so I snatched one up right away. I think I paid $750 (that I *really* didn't have at the time) for it.

Just like Robert Boatman's article, the information in that briefcase changed me. Up until that point, I really hadn't been exposed to direct response marketing principles. Listening to and watching each presentation helped me to visualize *exactly* how I could apply these powerful concepts to my own struggling business.

I proceeded to implement as many of these automated, direct response marketing principles as I could. I completely changed almost every aspect of my publishing business. These changes allowed me to transform and expand *Concealed Carry Magazine* into a strong and profitable organization (USCCA) in less than two years. Since then, the change and growth I've experienced—both personally and professionally—has been incredible.

So fast forward to that flight home from the NRA Meeting & Exhibits in Indiana in April 2014, where we had just given away almost five *thousand* copies of *Concealed Carry Magazine,* and it's easy to see why it felt like things had come full circle. In fact, I get a little choked up just thinking about it.

And the thing is, I know there's more to come. More good times, sure, and more bad times, too. But the important thing is to get in the game and keep pushing *forward*.

To be honest, *this book is about pushing forward.*

This book is also about faith. About what happens when you believe in something so unconditionally that the only way to go is up.

This book is about family. About loved ones who drive everything you do, and who you would do anything for.

But ultimately, this book is about freedom. About standing up for what you believe.

I hope that my story inspires *you* to keep pushing forward. I hope it inspires you to embrace and celebrate your faith, your family, and your freedom.

If you are someone who would do anything to protect the ones you love, thank you. This book is for you.

CHAPTER 2

ORDINARY & HUMBLE BEGINNINGS

I joined the USCCA for the peace of mind...knowing that if a
shooting incident happened, I would have the necessary help
available for all that would follow.

– Fran S., MN

I think I was a sophomore when I approached my dad and told him I wanted to play varsity football. I was on JV, and I thought I could do better.

He said, "Well, Tim, if you really want that, you need to follow the credo: *If it is to be, it's up to me.*"

As any normal teenager reacting to repeated advice would do, I rolled my eyes.

I'd heard this same phrase from Dad so many times before, but I waited for him to explain further. I had to admit: as much as I tended to brush off his reiteration, he was usually pretty good at giving me ways to apply it to a particular situation.

He said, "Here's what I want you to do. At your next JV game, I want you to pretend that all of your teammates are gone...that they've disappeared. When that ball gets kicked off, you're the *only* guy who can make that tackle. You have to believe that you are the only one on the field who can do it."

Despite the dubious look I'd given my dad, he *had* made a pretty good point. And the truth is, I was starting to realize more and more that he usually gave advice that worked.

So that next game, I put on my pads and my Roncalli Jets JV uniform and slid my helmet on, just like every other time. But I did something else: I played my dad's words over and over again in my head like I was watching game film. And then I did *exactly* what he suggested.

I'd never had a game like that before in my life. Even *I* didn't know what I was really capable of until that point. I mean, I knew I wasn't the fastest guy or the strongest guy on the team, but something about me was different in those minutes I spent on the field. It was intense. I visualized success, and it changed, quite literally, *everything*.

And my coach? Well, he noticed the change, too.

It was a "wow" moment for me—the first step in *really* understanding that my dad had some wisdom about things. It wasn't just me being obedient and going along with what he told me to do. It was different. I guess it just finally sunk in that my dad, man...he's really got some good stuff.

Now, I don't want to say that I took my dad for granted, as I think a lot of kids have a tendency to do when they're growing up, but I admit I never really gave our relationship much thought up until that point. I mean, sure...we lived in the same house, he was married to Mom, and he liked "dad stuff" and being in the garage, but I guess when you're fortunate enough to have your dad around as a kid—when you're fortunate enough to live a simple but good life—you don't spend too much time thinking about how lucky you are. Now, of course, I realize how special it was to have had that.

The easiest way to describe my childhood is to imagine the Cleaver family. We were about as typical as you could get: Ward, June, and the kids, though I also have a younger sister. It was my mom, Connie; my dad, Russ; my younger brother, Greg; and my sister, Julie. My dad worked in finance for a food processing company and my mom was a homemaker. That was pretty typical in the community where we grew up: the dads worked and the moms stayed home. It wasn't until we were a little older that Mom went back to work and taught Spanish.

We were a traditional family in every respect. My dad was—and is—a good man. He was the disciplinarian and expected as close to perfection as possible. The three of us kids tried really hard to meet his expectations. Sometimes we did...and sometimes we didn't. Mostly we just wanted his approval. I remember thinking, even back then, that there was *nothing* worse than disappointing my dad. (Seriously, disappointing him was *always* more crushing than the actual "screwing up" part.) To be honest, I was afraid of him until I was at least 22 or 23, and I still feel that same way about disappointing him. I guess some things never really change.

My mom was pretty much the polar opposite of my dad. She gave the hugs and kisses, and she kept every single Mother's Day card I ever made her. (In fact, every few years, I get an envelope in the mail of stuff like that from her.) She was—and still is—a very happy, grateful person. I actually wish I was a little more like her, because those are really good qualities to have. They can get you through a lot of tough stuff. My grandmother died when my mom was nine or 10, and though she ended up with a stepmother, it just deepened the relationship my mom had with her dad. (If I'm like anyone, I'm like him—my grandfather. He was a very successful businessman and was incredibly hard-working and focused. As a self-proclaimed "doer," I like to think I got a little bit of my drive from him.)

She was also the kind of mom who never really got mad. To this day, I've never seen her lose her temper. She came close sometimes. I remember Greg and I would screw around to the point where she would start yelling at us—well, her version of yelling, at least —and it took everything we had not to start laughing at her. We weren't trying to be cruel; we just knew that she'd be doling out love a few minutes later. But she did have a proverbial ace in the hole: when she told us she'd be telling Dad, we knew we were headed for the deep stuff.

Later in life, my parents told me that they actually had discussions away from us kids about discipline. So I know that they weren't always on the same page, but we always saw the united front. Mom felt all of our pain—from falling off our bicycles to skinning our knees to breaking curfew and knowing we'd spend the entire weekend in the house. Dad would tell us, "You're okay. Get up!" or "You knew the rules and decided to disobey them...and now you've got to pay the price." Mom never said anything in front of us, but she did advocate for us behind the scenes if she had a different perspective on what was going on.

That's not to say, however, that my dad didn't let loose once in awhile.

Case in point: the driving lessons he gave us when Greg and I were about four and five. (I'm sure the statute of limitations is up on this, so I can talk about it now.)

When we lived in Beaver Dam, my dad worked for Green Giant, a vegetable processing plant. We had a huge processing facility nearby that had huge paved parking lots and driveways all around the plant. The freshly picked vegetables would get delivered from the farms and then the semi-trucks would haul away the processed vegetables. So there was ample room for my dad to give me and Greg driving lessons, even if we were more than a decade from actually getting our licenses. We definitely saw them as legitimate, honest-to-God "driving lessons," because that's how my dad pitched them to us. In reality, we were sitting on his lap working the steering wheel while he took care of the gas pedal and brakes for us. I'd like to think that was merely a practical assist on his part: we simply weren't tall enough to see over the dashboard if we had to do that, too.

I also believe there was a bigger lesson in those illegal driving excursions. Could we just hop in and drive Dad's car anywhere? Of course not. We could only do this with his supervision and help; there was always guidance and practice and feedback. We had to drive between the lines! That's something a five-year-old can usually comprehend: *just keep the car between the lines.* (Well, at least *try* to keep the car between the lines!) Our "driving lessons" never really progressed beyond the Green Giant parking lot, but boy did we have fun steering that car around! We never got caught and it was a great experience to have with our dad.

THE GREEN GIANT T-SHIRTS

Dad used to take Greg and me to the Green Giant company store, which was where employees could buy company-branded products and other Green Giant items. Around the time that Dad was giving us our early driving lessons, I saw my first Green Giant t-shirt...and I knew I had to have one! So did Greg. We begged and begged for those t-shirts and got nowhere. No amount of whining or pleading was going to change Dad's mind. If it had been Mom, it would have been a totally different matter. We would have walked out of there wearing those t-shirts.

Dad said we'd have to earn the t-shirts if we really wanted them. Earn them? I was five. I had no concept of earning anything. Wasn't life about getting and receiving? Not according to Dad. Nobody just gave you things in his world. You had to work for them.

He was clever about that lesson, though. He created an exchange system where we worked doing extra chores around the house to earn stickers, which would ultimately get turned in for t-shirt credit. Now, really, what kind of chore can a five-year-old do that doesn't result in a bigger mess than when he started?

It had to have been a great early learning experience for me and Greg, but to be honest, all I remember about this was that I finally earned enough stickers to get that t-shirt!

My parents met and married in Minnesota, which is where they both were from. Mom was already a teacher, and Dad was in the Army Reserve. When he graduated from college, they moved to Beaver Dam, Wisconsin. You've probably never been to or heard of Beaver Dam; it's a quintessential American town. In the early

1970s, it had about 12,000 people and it was incredibly isolated geographically. That was good *and* bad. The good part is that it was an entirely self-sufficient community: barbershops and hair salons, meat markets and hardware stores, banks, car dealerships, and a hospital. We had everything we needed there. It was a very honest and humble community.

The bad? We were stuck in the middle of nowhere.

At our house in Beaver Dam, we actually had a white picket fence around the yard. Inside the house, we had an old Franklin wood stove that helped keep our heating bills down in the winter. We lived a very modest lifestyle—used cars (usually old station wagons to haul us around) and hand-me-down clothes—and while we didn't really want for anything, there wasn't a lot of money left over for unnecessary things. My mom cooked everything; we always sat down for meals. She even did some canning, which is ironic seeing as Dad worked for Green Giant at the time. We'd go out to dinner maybe three times a year—once for each kid's birthday—which was a very big deal to us. We'd go to Pizza Hut or some place similar. We were really living large.

MY PARENTS AND THEIR
SUNDAY NIGHT PIZZA

Now that we're grown and out of the house, my mom and dad actually go out for pizza every Sunday. They have a local place they like to go to and they're regulars there.

One Sunday, they're sitting at the bar and talking to this guy. (My parents live in a friendly community, and that's not all that unusual.) The conversation continues on, and it becomes clear they are of a similar mindset. People around town know who my dad is and who I am, but this guy doesn't. They start talking about concealed carry and the guy suggests that my dad join this great association, one that he really thinks my dad would like.

Because of the way my dad is sitting, the guy can't see his USCCA shirt. (He has one, and he wears it regularly.) So my dad swivels around, points to his shirt, and says, "You mean this one?" The guy can't believe it! He's sitting next to Tim Schmidt's dad.

The three of us kids, while we all had different personalities and interests, actually had a pretty good childhood. Sure, we got into spats and arguments like all siblings do, but we did get along. In fact, Greg works for the USCCA, so I must've been a fairly decent big brother for him to want to work here with me. We don't go out for Pizza Hut though; he works in our Utah office.

I was the first-born child, and I think I was pretty typical. I was the one bushwhacking the way for the other two who followed. If we did get in trouble, I was the one who should have known better—purely because I was older, and therefore naturally more responsible. Or at least I *should* have been. First-borns, you know what I'm talking about: it's impossible to catch a break on that one, no matter how much you want to try to argue it.

If my parents expected perfection from me, that's what I would do. It just sort of came naturally to me. I was always a high achiever in that respect. I didn't really feel the need to question it. It became my goal, and I was never really content with doing anything halfway. Even as a little kid, I was 100% "in." It didn't necessarily mean I always achieved what I set out to, but I sure tried hard.

Describing the way I grew up in the '70s and '80s probably sounds like just about any other household in the Midwest. If we misbehaved, our names went up on the back of the kitchen door... and if we did something wrong, we'd do the dishes or some other chore for recompense. We had structure and discipline. After we finished eating, we asked to be excused.

We attended mass every weekend. In fact, we were usually the first people at church, typically 20 minutes early, always sitting in the same pew. We attended Catholic school. That's just what we did. It wasn't something we really thought about.

Mom and Dad never fought in front of us. It's actually interesting to look back now and think about how well the two of them complemented each other—as parents and as a couple. I think part of that compatibility is what you find attractive in another person, but part of it also comes from years of being together. You learn each other's strengths and weaknesses. You pick your battles. You find ways to make things work. Mom and Dad? They always found a way to make things work.

Nope...they never fought in front of us, and they never talked money in front of us, either. We were certainly never wealthy, and like many families in the Midwest, we were frugal and lived below our means. That certainly had an impact on us.

But my mom and dad also taught us things that were much more intangible. Living frugally is fairly easy for a kid to figure out: buying a used car costs less than a new car. Only going out to eat three times a year, which adds up when you have a family, means that you can save money for better meals at home. Cause and effect is pretty simple. When you spend less than you earn, you can build yourself a nest egg for emergencies.

Then there was the harder stuff to understand as a kid: what you want is there for the taking, but you have to work for it. Opportunity is everywhere, but you need to be creative in figuring out how to use it. That required work.

On top of that, my dad also taught us the "abundance mentality," about being grateful for what you have. I have to admit: sometimes that's hard when you're a kid and there are classmates who live in bigger, better houses with bigger, better toys and who go off to Disney while you go camping. But this was an important idea for my dad, and one that he worked with us on to really understand: the more you are grateful for, the more you will *have* to be grateful for. If you are happy and truly appreciate what you have, more opportunities will present themselves to you.

Those are some pretty complex ideas for a kid to grasp, but Dad had a way of putting things into words we could understand. For example, if we wanted something, we had to earn the money to buy it. (Our Green Giant t-shirts were just the beginning…) The best part was that our parents gave us the latitude to try to make that money.

From a very young age, we just "got it." In fact, my first foray into business was actually a partnership with my brother, Greg. We were just kids at the time, but we could think big! We had a great idea—to sell crayfish to the local fishermen in Waunakee, another small Wisconsin town we lived in before moving to Manitowoc.

On the surface, it wasn't that bad of an idea. We had a virtually unlimited supply of crayfish at our disposal and a willing market to buy them. The biggest variable was labor, and we were both gung-ho about our idea.

So we headed down to Six Mile Creek with the intent to catch as many crayfish as possible. And we caught what we thought had to be a truckload. We hauled them back home, dragged my sister's swimming pool out into the yard, and dumped them in. Marketing wasn't that big of an issue, but properly pricing our product was. After some discussion, we thought that 50 cents a dozen was a fair price. We were going to live the high life, make a killing…corner the crayfish market in Waunakee, Wisconsin.

Our first customer stepped up, checked out our pool, and asked how much we were charging. The price was definitely right…and he placed an order for two dozen.

And that was when Greg and I realized we'd only caught 17 crayfish. Our first customer had put us out of business.

My second "business" was already set up for me when I took it over. When I was 10 years old, I had the opportunity to inherit a paper route. Being a paperboy is kind of like being an entrepreneur in that you really are your own boss. There's no one looking over your shoulder. I liked that freedom, so I was all over that opportunity.

I needed money. I had my eye on a new bike: a Schwinn 10 Speed. I was all jacked up at the prospect. It was my first *real* business opportunity; the crayfish business was just practice.

While my entrepreneurial nature kicked in pretty early, my business acumen took a little longer to flourish. I didn't really understand the concept behind the paper route, and the kid never really explained it to me when he handed it over. An entire year went by with me diligently collecting money and turning it into the newspaper. (Back then, when you had a route, you collected money from your customers, and then you had to turn it over at the depot where you picked up the papers.)

For some reason, I thought that being a paperboy meant that you were supposed to get paid at some point. You know...with a *real* paycheck. This was a real job, right? Real jobs mean paychecks! I mean, my dad got a paycheck. I guess I just assumed I would too. So I would go to the depot, pay my money, and just stand there. But every week, they ignored me. Eventually I would just leave...*without* a paycheck. I was Timid Tim, too uncomfortable to ask what the deal was.

My dad checked in with me often during those first few months to see how I was doing. As much as he was good at giving me space to make my own decisions (and mistakes), he wasn't really going to let me sink. I had been reluctant to tell him about my problems at first because I had not come to grips with them. I was confused. Were they forgetting to pay me? Would there come a day when I was standing there, getting in the way, and they finally remembered that stack of checks they were forgetting to hand over to me? I had to come clean. He listened patiently, asked a few questions, and then finally said, "Well, you wanted this job so you could afford a new bike. It's your route and you know what you have to do." Essentially, he pulled out the "If it is to be, it's up to me."

It would have been nothing for him to storm into the depot and raise a ruckus on my behalf, but what would I have learned from that? He probably knew how a paper route worked, and could have figured out my problem for me, but then it wouldn't be my paper route anymore. It would be a paper route he managed for me. We didn't work that way. It wasn't, "If it is to be, it's up to Dad."

I delivered the paper for an entire year without making any profit. I eventually figured out that there were people on the route who had essentially been getting the newspaper for free—not just from me, but also from the kid who gave me the paper route. They'd gotten the paper free for years and had never said anything.

After that first year, and that talk with my dad, I fixed the paper route. Actually, I did *more* than fix it. I had the fundamentals of income over expense under control at that point, and I started cold calling for new customers. Timid Tim went door-to-door selling newspaper subscriptions. I explained the convenience of having a newspaper delivered and promised it would be high and dry, on time, and right on their first step. It took about a year, but I managed to get paid for all the papers I was delivering. Plus, I had increased the route from 36 to 72 subscribers. I had positive cash flow and, as a well-managed route, it was yielding some decent money. I had solved a major problem.

That's something I've always been good at: if there's a problem, I like to solve it—often in a way that makes little sense to others. I guess that's just the way I think—the engineer in me. See, engineers like to make things complex, but that's not always the best way to execute things. I've learned that the hard way, and it's something I continue to work on.

It's also a skill to know when to move on. That crayfish business? Not worth it. Now *that* was a flawed business model if I'd ever seen one. It was extremely labor intensive and inventory would be a perpetual problem. Plus, eventually my sister would have wanted her pool back.

With the paper route, I figured out that I was supposed to collect more money than I turned in, and that was profit for me. That was my paycheck. Eventually, I actually doubled the size of my route, which helped me to make the money I needed. When I had the $179, I went and bought that Schwinn I'd had my eye on.

I eventually gave up my paper route when I got to high school. I had my sights set on something better. A new grocery store had opened up about a mile and a half from our house. My dad had worked at a grocery store as a teenager growing up in Glencoe, Minnesota, and he had told me stories about his days working there.

It always sounded like fun, so I decided my next job would be at Food Country, the new local store. I found out who the manager was and went over and talked to him. There weren't any openings, but he said he'd keep me in mind.

You have to realize that a lot of the lessons I learned as a kid I learned through experience. My dad was always able and willing to guide us, but these were things we did on our own. However, when it came to my first real chance at employment, my dad politely stepped in and suggested I visit the Food Country guy every week until he hired me. It sounded like good advice to me.

I took it upon myself to check in every single week from that point on. It got to the point where I would say, "Just keep me in mind for the next opening," and the manager would respond with something like, "Trust me kid, you'll be the first one I'll call."

I probably got the job because he was sick of me showing up like clockwork every week. My persistence wore him down. I don't give up easily at all. I never have.

I started out as a stocker and really enjoyed it. I liked stocking and facing; I liked—and still like—to just get stuff done. I'm really competitive, and I like jobs where you can see the work you've done and how it compares to other people doing the same work.

Eventually I worked my way up to being a cashier, which was an even better job than stocking. There was still that sense of getting things done, of competition, but I was the only male cashier among a whole schedule of high school girls. It was a great job in many, many ways.

When we were growing up, we always felt loved and supported, and not just with our entrepreneurial adventures. That was important to my parents, and clear to us. My dad is a pretty tough guy, and yet he did a pretty good job of talking with us. One thing Dad didn't say a whole lot was "I love you," but when I look back, he didn't need to. He showed us he loved us through his actions. He never missed our activities; he was always at my football games. He supported us in everything. So did my mom.

I learned a lot from him, both as a dad and through what he did professionally. My dad had worked his way up through the finance department in a food processing company—accountant, then controller, then CFO—and he really understood accounting automation, which was a new innovation back then. When I was in sixth grade or so, he decided to take what he knew and start his own business on the side. He was an expert in what he did, and he knew that knowledge could help other companies. By that time, we'd moved to Manitowoc, Wisconsin, where there were other food processing companies.

He had a great idea, and he really knew what he was doing. But his business plan had a fatal flaw: because he was still working full time and had his successful career, he hired someone full time in the new business. That person was the one who cultivated the relationships and eventually stole the business from him. He felt so bad when it happened, and the thing is, that person he hired still has a successful business in the community.

My dad taught me, through what he said and what he did, that with hard work, disciplined risk taking, and a positive mental attitude, you could achieve anything. When I look back on that, I realize I believed him and I still do.

When people see where I am now—president and founder of the USCCA (an organization focused completely on the responsibly armed American)—it's easy to see why they assume I grew up in a "hunting" family or at least one where guns were the foundation of our family culture. That's not true. Sure, we had guns, but they weren't the focal point by any means.

In some ways, though, I think my childhood was not all that different from many USCCA members. When it really comes down to it, I think the values I grew up with, and the values of the USCCA community, are pretty much the same. If you're reading this book, I bet a lot of my childhood sounds familiar to you: the importance of family, of hard work, of doing the right thing. I have to admit: now that I'm a dad, I'm trying to instill those same values into *my* kids.

You have to remember that I grew up in a conservative family in a conservative community. Surprisingly, *not* owning a gun was fairly atypical in the community I grew up in. If you went door-to-door in Beaver Dam or Manitowoc back then—and probably even now—I bet the majority of the people who answered their doors would tell you they owned at least one gun, just as we did. This was a culture where there were often guns in the house "just in case." If something happened, you needed to protect yourself, end of discussion. It's really not something that anyone gave much thought to when I was growing up. It wasn't a big deal. You didn't really talk about it or brag that your family had a gun or guns, particularly if you were a hunting family. It was neither good nor bad. It just was, and you respected it as a kid.

I also grew up in Wisconsin. We're a hunting state, so inevitably people had guns for that. Deer hunting is a major holiday in Wisconsin—families call their kids in absent to school and generations of hunters go out in the fields and hunt together. Bars throw parties for "deer hunter widows" during hunting season. There's a reason why, if you catch a Green Bay Packers home game on television, green and gold evolves into blaze orange the more the temperature drops. Those blaze orange jackets are constructed to keep you warm while you sit in a deer stand for hours on end. It's the warmest clothing many Wisconsin residents own.

But me? I've never been much of a hunter. My dad didn't hunt, so I didn't really get into it either. But that didn't mean there weren't guns around when I was growing up!

My dad had actually been in the Army Reserve during Vietnam, and he had guns. We would go to the range and shoot as a recreational activity. It was about marksmanship. He'd learned that skill in the military and he just kept it up.

We also had a BB gun, which was very typical back then. As long as I didn't shoot anyone, I was allowed to take it out and shoot at targets and soda cans.

My mom, of course, wanted to shelter us. She was very overprotective. But really, that wasn't any fun. We understood that BB guns had power and could be dangerous, but during the summer, we pretty much free-ranged with ours.

As we got older, Mom's concern never really went away. We'd run down to the edge of town with the BB gun and put pop bottles and cans on hay bales. The irony is that I can't ever remember us doing anything stupid with that BB gun. Our dad's lessons and emphasis on gun safety were always in the back of our heads. We took his words seriously. There was nothing funny about aiming a gun at someone, even when you absolutely, positively knew it wasn't loaded (because you *never* took that chance). We just never questioned anything Dad taught us about guns. We knew better.

To be honest, we saved stupid for the chemistry set and for seeing how big of a hole we could blow in the ground with fireworks. (My favorite experiment? Seeing how many fireworks we could tie together to make that hole.) Seriously, who *wouldn't* do that if they had the chance?

I've followed the same philosophy with my own kids that my dad used with us regarding guns. It's not a gun safe or a gun lock that will keep your kids safe; it's education and knowledge. You may take the time to properly lock up your guns, but someday your kids will find themselves in a home where someone doesn't. So then it's a matter of what you've taught them. You have to take the time to teach them, to give them supervised access, to take the thrill out of it a little. Disrespecting a gun is no different than disrespecting a power saw—if you don't respect the saw, you'll cut your fingers off. If you don't respect what can happen with a gun, you or someone else could end up dead. It's pretty simple.

Take the time to teach that lesson to your kids, make sure they really understand it, and they'll develop the right respect to stay safe.

THE FUN IN SCHMIDT FAMILY VACATIONS

We did a lot of camping when I was a kid. Early on, our camping was not campground camping—with inside bathrooms and electric and water connections at a campsite—but real deep woods camping out in the wild with no one else around. We would drive along unpaved forest roads—which still exist in some parts of northern Wisconsin—and then after we parked our station wagon, we'd hike into the woods even farther. (If there were cell phones back then, we'd be at negative bars.) After that, we'd clear a campsite and literally set up camp. We'd pitch our tent, unroll our sleeping bags, build a fire ring, gather firewood, make accommodations for our food so that it was "bear proof" (which often meant getting it up in a tree where they couldn't reach it), and figure out where to fish if we were near a creek or a river. It takes work to make a campsite into a temporary home and keep it that way. In later years, these trips became more civilized, and Dad would rent a cabin for a week. But this really wasn't a vacation in the kick-back-and-relax sense. We still had chores. Being on vacation was no excuse to be irresponsible.

It's funny because these were never hunting trips, but my dad was always armed. Cell phones were still more than two decades from a practical reality; 911 existed, but who exactly would come help us in the middle of nowhere even if we managed to call them? It wasn't like we could give them any sort of address. Can you imagine? "Look for our car on the dirt road and then walk south for about a half hour and turn left at the creek and we're somewhere about 20 minutes from there near the white pines."

Really, our biggest threat up there was a bear. Most bears don't like humans and don't want to be around humans, but there was always a chance that we could startle one or cross paths with a bear and her cubs. Bears are hungry creatures who can smell food; usually when a bear ends up in your campsite, it's a mission for food. But bears also aren't going to stop for you to run to your car or call for help. You're just an inconvenience, standing in the way of dinner, or you're just a little too close to her cubs (even if that's an accidental thing on your part). Even now, bear sightings in Wisconsin's Northwoods are fairly common. So our vacations always included my dad's Smith & Wesson .357, which he kept on his hip.

My dad always made a point of taking the three of us kids out on one-on-one vacations with him. They weren't anything big or extravagant; the special part was that it was just time to spend alone with Dad. We'd go rafting or canoeing or some other fun activity. He always took his gun with him, too, for protection.

When I was about 11, my dad took me on a camping trip in the Wisconsin Northwoods. For those who have never been to northern Wisconsin, it's still a beautiful area: quite pristine and a great place for people who enjoy the outdoors. The fact that he took a gun with him was actually smart—there are bears and other wild animals up there. Though rare, there are also cougars and bobcats in Wisconsin—not to mention wolves and elk. Parts of it are so isolated that it wouldn't seem out of place to encounter Big Foot.

As part of this particular camping trip, he made a point of finding a nearby shooting range. And this was the trip where my dad let me hold his Smith & Wesson .357 Magnum—and let me shoot it for the very first time.

Now, this is a big revolver. And it's nickel plated. He still has it, and it's beautiful. To this day, he still babies that gun.

But I will never forget when he pulled it out. It was far from the BB gun I had used on the soda cans. I was a little nervous, but boy, was I excited, too. This was a real gun, and a big gun for an 11-year-old boy to handle. I was surprised that he would let me shoot his super-cool Smith & Wesson, but he knew I respected it. How? Because he did exactly what all parents should do: he taught us that a gun is not a toy or a novelty or something thrilling to check out when Mom and Dad are out of the house. My dad trusted me. That's something profound, something not lost on a young boy.

As most shooters know, you can shoot two types of ammunition in this revolver: .38 Special and .357 Magnum. He started me with the .38, which is pretty powerful on its own. And then he offered to let me try out the .357.

Holy smokes...that was *awesome.*

I remember feeling so important. My dad trusted me to shoot his gun. Me, an 11-year-old kid. It was heavy—or at least a lot heavier than our BB gun—and it produced some serious recoil.

But it was something I quickly adjusted to and we spent the afternoon at the range. Every kid should have the opportunity to do that with his or her dad.

That's really how I knew our parents—especially my dad—loved us. He didn't say it all the time, but he always showed it. Dad didn't need to take us on those trips. He and Mom could have done something on their own. He could have used his vacation time from work to get stuff done around the house or just kick back and take it easy. And yet, he paid attention to us and took time to be with us. He and my mom were always there when we needed them.

Both my parents were very supportive of the decisions I made growing up. Sure, I didn't always make the best choices, but kids need the opportunity to make mistakes—to find out what they're good (and not so good) at. Sports are a perfect example. You may want to play a certain sport, but you don't necessarily have the skills, the drive, or even the right body type to do it. But if it's something you really want to do, why not try? Putting yourself out there and seeing how far you can go is sometimes worth the challenge—and the experience. My parents saw the value in letting us try a lot of things, even if those things didn't end up being the right "fit" for us.

I did naturally excel at a few things—science, math, football—and other things I just did as a challenge. Take basketball: I really wasn't very good and I knew it. But what I did have was an unending drive to push myself harder than everyone else. I guess that's just part of my personality. (And honestly, my intense drive made up for a *lot*...in fact, it still does.)

THE LONGEST TIMEOUT OF MY HIGH SCHOOL CAREER

Whenever I get to a point in my life where I am in need of some motivation, I think back to Mr. Geigel, my basketball coach. I didn't particularly like him, but that didn't mean he wouldn't have a pretty profound influence on me. He was one of the most intimidating people I had ever met. As our coach, he spent most of his time yelling at us, and—to be honest—I was a little scared of him.

I'll never forget one specific game against our biggest conference rival. My team wasn't playing badly, but we certainly weren't playing well. We were slow, and clumsy, and no one was really pushing to make a big play. So Coach Geigel called a timeout.

Now, a timeout in basketball lasts only 30 seconds. And I have to tell you, Coach Geigel sat down in the middle of our huddle and looked every single one of us straight in the eye. And he didn't say a word for 28 seconds. Instead of telling us to hustle more or put more heart into it, he just stared at us.

It was 28 seconds of complete silence. It felt like the longest 28 seconds of my entire life.

And then, right before we headed back onto the court, his face turned bright red. He clenched his fists and shouted, "GET IN THE GAME!"

You can imagine what happened next. The game changed completely.

High school was a big turning point for me. Growing up, I had a temper problem. I didn't have a lot of friends. I was the new kid in fourth grade, and being new is a big deal when you're a kid. It got me a handful of friends, but by eighth grade I didn't have *any*. I wasn't very nice to be around, to be honest. It's still a little painful to look back at those years.

It took me awhile, but I recognized I had a problem, and so I went to my dad for help. He had me listen to tapes: Zig Ziglar and Dale Carnegie's *How to Win Friends and Influence People*. And I did listen to them. Seriously, I did. I was so desperate to have friends that I ended up brainwashing myself and buying into everything Ziglar and Carnegie said. But that was a good thing. I listened to the tapes every day. I taught myself how to be a good friend. I reprogrammed how I thought and acted. I believed in what these guys were saying to me on these tapes. (I had to; I didn't really have any other options at that point.)

Zig Ziglar is a great person to read or listen to if you need general inspiration. He was a consummate salesperson, and I believe his self-motivational advice can help anyone overcome inherent shyness, reluctance, or self-defeating thoughts. He was also quite funny. He professed there were no shortcuts to success—only hard work. It was basically what my dad had been telling me all along, but I was hearing it from someone else. (If you're a parent, you know the phenomenon: things tend to "sink in" more when someone *other* than you says them!)

I also listened to Norman Vincent Peale. He was a theologian and a psychologist who professed the power of positive thinking in self-development.

These men are no longer alive, but they are still highly regarded, and I recommend their works for anyone to study. I still don't really know why my dad bought all those tapes for me. At the time, I didn't realize just how much he was helping me. But I'm grateful he did, because to be honest, I attribute a lot of my long-term successes to the hours I spent listening to those tapes as a teenager.

Getting to high school and being able to go out for football—well, I was set to excel at anything that required me to be strong and stubborn. The timing was perfect, too. I had been listening to the tapes my dad gave me and trying to be a different person, one who was actually likeable. And there was a new mix of kids in high school, because we were all coming from different schools. This gave me the opportunity to try out some of those things that I had been listening to day in and day out. And it worked—a lot of those people who grew to dislike me in middle school started to like me in high school. Heck, some of those same people became my closest friends.

I continued to play different sports, which also helped me meet new people. I also excelled at biology and chemistry. There weren't too many of my fellow football players getting A's with me in my advanced science classes! I got to know the head of the science department quite well. His name was Mr. Soquet. He was a tough and mostly fair teacher. But as a senior, I made the decision *not* to take Mr. Soquet's Advanced Chemistry class. My parents completely supported me, but that decision blacklisted me with Mr. Soquet.

I had taken a lot of science, including chemistry and math, and it opened up my eyes to what I could do as an engineer. It was something that appealed to me. It was really right up my alley.

Plus, it was another option that didn't involve Advanced Chemistry. I was convinced I could succeed without that class!

Now this was also at the point in high school where I started to pay attention during career day...but I can tell you that my interest in engineering had absolutely nothing to do with what I learned from the engineer who came to talk to us. In fact, his presentation was so dull that it was surprising that any of us sustained an interest in engineering at all. The guy held up a paper clip and talked about how it was the kind of thing an engineer designed on a regular basis—how that was typical of what engineers do. The takeaway from his presentation was pretty easy to figure out: being an engineer really sucked.

But I was already headstrong and confident in myself, and I knew I wanted to be an engineer. I had a bit of a problem, though. My grades in high school were modest—about two-thirds Bs and the rest As. I took standard high school classes and a few advanced mathematics and science classes, but I knew it was going to be ultra competitive out there. My grades didn't exactly match my abilities, my IQ, or my drive.

Engineering was a good fit for me. When I look back, it really made sense, but I probably didn't completely realize it at the time. Engineers really don't have a lot of interaction with people; they're focused on problem solving and creating solutions. I was, despite teaching myself how to be a better friend to people, still inherently a shy person who was far more interested in getting things done than establishing relationships. I wasn't quite Timid Tim anymore, but I was far from being a social butterfly. Back then, though, I just thought it was a cool career for me. And I ended up receiving an academic scholarship from Michigan Tech to study engineering.

The funny thing was, at graduation, the person designated to give me my scholarship was Mr. Soquet. When he handed it to me, he leaned toward me and said, "You'll never make it at Michigan Tech."

Which is exactly the thing you *don't* say to someone like me.

What Mr. Soquet had meant as an insult fueled my drive to succeed—to show him that he was completely off base about me. How much did that inspire me? It's almost 25 years later and I still think about him and what he said. I continue to prove him wrong. Talk about the power and impact a teacher has over a student! My dad drilled into me, and into my brother and sister, though, that whether or not we were successful was up to *us*—not some disgruntled chemistry teacher. No one was in charge of what we could do except *us*.

I thought I'd have a few months of freedom before I actually headed up to Michigan Tech. Graduation was behind me and there was one last summer with my buddies to look forward to at that point.

My parents were always super strict with us, and we always had a curfew (of course, mine was always earlier than that of my buddies). We had to "check in" when we got home because Mom would be awake and waiting for us. You know, I don't even really think it was to catch us to make sure we were sober or anything like that. I think Mom just genuinely wanted to make sure we'd made it safely home and to say goodnight.

So you can probably imagine how thrilled I was when my dad appeared in my basement bedroom and announced that now that I was an adult and a high school graduate, I no longer had a curfew. There would be no more rules to follow.

My immediate thought? *This is going to be the BEST summer ever!*

But he continued. He said I could stay at home through the summer before I headed off to Michigan Tech. At that point, I shouldn't plan on living at home anymore. And he and Mom would pay my first semester of college...but after that, I was on my own. (Michigan Tech runs on a trimester schedule, so that meant I was taken care of until…Thanksgiving. Ouch.)

My second thought? Absolute dread. I went from elation to utter fear in just a few seconds. Yeah, sure, I'd gotten the scholarship, but it wasn't enough. I was over a barrel. This wasn't how I'd hoped to spend my summer at all.

I took the practical route and found myself a factory job, working second shift all summer in a corrugated box factory without air conditioning. I worked from 2 p.m. until 10 p.m. every day and usually rolled in about 4 a.m. or 5 a.m. after hanging out with my buddies. If my mom was up, it was probably because she was getting ready to start her day. On one hand, it was probably a relief for her not to stay up while I was out. On the other hand, I could see her *not* getting a great night's sleep (because she was worried about what I was doing). She was still my mom, after all.

The place where I worked hired on a crew of college kids every summer and, of course, they saved the lousiest jobs that nobody wanted for us. But that's how those jobs usually go, so it didn't really bother me at all. I knew I could work harder than all the people there, and I did.

In fact, my first night on the job, there was a guy that was just mean-mugging me all through the shift from across the floor. He finally came over to me during break and said, "I got one thing to say to you. Slow the f*** down. You're making us all look bad." That was my introduction to the union mentality. Of course, I didn't. Honestly, I probably worked just a little faster from that point on.

Already at that age, I was hearing my dad's words echo in my head: "If it is to be, it's up to me." I was going to go to Michigan Tech, I was going to make that money to pay for it, and I was going to be an engineer.

CHAPTER 3

HIT LIKE A LIGHTNING BOLT

I joined the USCCA because my family is very special and dear to me. Protecting them is utmost in my mind. For years I was searching for an organization that offers a complete package: education, training, and an emphasis on safety...not only for myself but for my entire family. Real scenarios that all of us can relate to. USCCA offers everything that my family needed. Thank you for being there.

– Robert K., CA

My life-changing moment came at a time when I was about as defenseless as possible: buckled into an airplane seat, 30,000 feet above the earth. If something was to go wrong, there wasn't a darn thing I could do about it.

I'd just become a father, and Tim Jr. and Tonnie were waiting for me back home. I honestly don't remember where I was flying from, but when I wasn't mindlessly looking out the window, I was passing the time reading something.

Okay, it wasn't just something. If you're a member of the USCCA, you know what it was: "The Constitutional Right and Social Obligation to Carry a Gun" by the late Robert Boatman.

And if you haven't personally read it, you should.

FROM AUTHOR TO FRIEND

It's still kind of strange to me when people recognize me. But over the years, I've shared a lot of personal things—stories, struggles, successes—with USCCA members, so they've come to really know me and my family. I guess sometimes I forget that. We are all part of a really unique, close-knit community that exists in addition to where I actually live. That's kind of cool when you think about it. It's like having neighbors who live all around the country.

Obviously, at gun shows, people know who I am and I expect that. It doesn't seem like a long time, but USCCA members have really known me for more than a decade now. It's entirely reasonable that people recognize me outside of gun shows and the magazine. The members who were here at the beginning have seen me go from this guy with a crazy awesome idea to start Concealed Carry Magazine *and build an association to Tactical Tim—which was sort of a larger-than-life personality that I took on for a while in the magazine—to now just Tim. It's been great. I'm happy being just Tim.*

One time, I was in Washington, D.C. and I was getting something to eat and this guy came up to me out of nowhere and said, "Hey! You're Tactical Tim!"

Well, yes, that's me. And he recognized me when I was putting ketchup on my burger. It was cool. I was probably just as excited to see him as he was to see me, because it was so unexpected for both of us. I wish I knew his name because I would definitely give him a shout out here.

Hey buddy, if you're reading this, that was a pretty cool moment for me too!

At one point, I was sitting on a plane reading Robert Boatman's writing, and just a few years later, I actually went on to meet and become friends with him before he died in 2009. We printed his work in Concealed Carry Magazine *too.*

It's pretty cool when you can actually meet someone who has influenced you in some big or even some small way. So I do understand how people are happy to meet me and share their stories. I had someone make a difference in my life, and it was Robert Boatman.

So, I was on this plane and I just had some reading material along to pass the time. I get bored and restless on flights; it's hard for me to sit still. I had brought along Boatman's writing and just thought it might keep me occupied until we landed in Milwaukee. Boy, was I wrong. I don't know what it really was—that I was missing my family or that it was just the right time and my mind was in the right place—but *wow.*

I was sitting there reading, and it just hit me like a lightning bolt: it was *my* responsibility to protect my family. I had a new little baby back home, and a wife, and they were sitting in Muskego, Wisconsin, which is about as "un-dangerous" of a small American town as you can get. Sometimes we would even forget to lock our front door. But bad things can and do happen where and when you least expect them. There's no sign at the outskirts of Muskego telling bad guys to stay out. And even if there was, they'd ignore it anyway.

I thought back to my dad and how having a gun in our house was a given. And time jumped ahead and I realized that *I* was now the dad, and my house was different. I had nothing to protect myself or my family. Dad was always prepared if something bad happened. And I wasn't. That realization blew my mind.

It was more than just owning a gun, too. It was a mindset. There was no question in my mind that if he needed to, my dad would have been right in front of Mom and us kids, defending us in a bad situation. It's not a situation he would have ever wanted to encounter, but when push came to shove, he'd do it. He felt that obligation right down to his core.

Now it wasn't just that I didn't own a gun. Was I falling down as a dad? As a husband?

I remember shifting uncomfortably in my seat. I'm a tall guy and airplane seats are uncomfortable to begin with, but this was something completely different.

Boatman wrote, "Carrying a gun is a social responsibility."

Wait...what? Come on.

Sure, I had grown up with a Smith & Wesson in the house. But a social responsibility? Sure, cops carry guns. But the average citizen? Man, this guy had some ballsy ideas. I was intrigued.

I kept reading: "A citizen who shirks his duty to contribute to the security of his community is little better than the criminal who threatens it."

Okay, now *that* blew my mind.

My dad had taught me so many things, but this was something I hadn't realized until I was sitting there on that plane. It all made sense suddenly. My dad would never have come out and told me to go buy a gun to protect my family. That just wasn't how he operated. He left it up to me to figure it out. And I was figuring it out, on a plane, with the help of Robert Boatman.

It astounded me. What Boatman was saying was hitting me hard. I had never thought that carrying a gun was really *that* important. No one had ever told me that I wasn't responsible. But if the good guys aren't responsible, who is? Who is responsible for protecting your family? It's *you*.

That was a profound idea. It's still a profound idea. Even writing about this, I still feel exactly how I felt on that flight. That has never left me.

I kept reading even more. I ate up what Boatman was saying. His words were harsh, but harsh in an important way. There was no sugar coating any of it. It really did just blow my mind.

Something changed in me, right there, on that airplane. I needed to do *something* to protect them, to protect us, as a family. That was MY responsibility first. It was more than that, too. It was like everything came together—all the life lessons I'd learned so far, all the times I'd picked myself up, even bits and pieces of what I learned as a kid. It hadn't completely come together until that moment.

It was something that resonated with me right down to the core. And if it was to be, it was up to me. That simple notion that I had heard all my life…it just made perfect sense at that point.

I threw away all the fear and the blame and the excuses. There wasn't any doubt I could do this. After God, the thing that mattered most to me was protecting my family.

I couldn't wait to land, to get off that airplane, and to get started.

And then reality hit.

Let's just say that my eagerness wasn't appreciated by the first person I went to for help. I went to a major big-box sporting goods store and went straight back to the gun counter, where there were some big guns.

It may seem hard to believe, but I'm still not naturally outgoing, especially with people I don't know. I admire people who have that gift of being able to comfortably strike up a conversation with anyone. There's still a part of me that hesitates. I'm not the timid kid who hung around the newspaper depot painfully waiting for someone to talk to him about his missing paycheck, but I'm also still not the guy who will talk your ear off in a waiting room. (If you ever happen to be sitting next to me on an airplane, the good news is that you'll never have to put your earbuds in and pretend to sleep to get me to stop talking.)

I've taught myself and learned how to interact with people and, while I do get nervous, I'm a lot more comfortable initiating a conversation. But do I like it? I'm still a pretty shy guy inside. That fundamentally has never quite changed, even in a situation like this one, where my hair was basically on fire about arming myself. I still didn't have it in me to charge into that store, hunt down someone in the firearms department, pepper him (or her) with questions, and walk out of there with a handgun in under 10 minutes.

That was very frustrating.

I was standing there looking at the guns, not really knowing who to ask for help, and—even more importantly—*what* to really ask the person who I hoped would steer me in the right direction. Finally, some employee wandered over and when I started talking to him about a specific gun, he said, "What would you need something like that for?"

It wasn't the response I had expected. I finally stammered something and walked away. I had absolutely no confidence in what I desperately felt the need to do. It was something I would encounter more than once on my journey to the USCCA. The existing gun culture was not all that welcoming to an outsider.

That's the reaction a big guy like me got. So what about a guy who *didn't* look like me—who looked a million years away from being a "gun owner?" Most of our USCCA members are men, but women answer that call too. Imagine what kind of reaction a woman who also felt the need to protect her family would have gotten from that employee. Would he have helped her? Or would she have been patronized to the point of leaving? People who carry, and who want to take on this responsibility, come in all shapes and sizes, but we all have one thing in common. And that day, in that store, no one but me seemed to take it seriously.

Although I didn't have a lot of practical experience at that point, I wasn't uncomfortable with guns. So it wasn't about starting from square one for me. I couldn't imagine how someone with no knowledge of guns who wanted to protect his or her family would do in my situation. How would someone who was starting at the very beginning fare? They'd likely run into the same irritating difficulties that I did.

That first gun shop experience didn't stop me, but it did frustrate me. I was already hooked on my idea. I needed to learn exactly how to do this as fast as possible, even if nobody wanted to help me. And so I started buying books and magazines about guns and shooting.

That's when I hit another roadblock. Most of the gun publications that existed at the time were about hunting and target shooting. There were articles on reloading ammunition and competition sights—interesting topics on their own, and I read them, but...*not* what I was looking for—and I was quickly frustrated: not by what was out there, but by what *wasn't* out there.

Sure, there were ammunition tests, but they were comparing 180-grain vs. 200-grain 300 Winchester Magnum cartridges, not defensive pistol ammunition. I learned all about holsters for police officers on patrol duty, but was still in the dark on what kind of holster was best for carrying a concealed firearm.

My library of information kept growing and becoming more complex and confusing. It was hard to keep track of, because what little information was helpful was in bits and pieces. My stack of gun magazines was getting taller and I was checking online forums and websites about concealed carry. It was a topic that did come up, but I couldn't find a single resource that focused 100 percent on defensive firearms and concealed carry.

It was irritating: all this stuff was out there, but it was missing the most critical component. There was nothing about or for the *people* who carried. Nothing about why people carried or how they carried or what happened in their lives that made them decide to become armed citizens.

What else was missing? For starters...*any* sort of discussion about the legal issues associated with concealed carry and self-defense. Arming yourself is something you need to think about and take seriously; it's not just about carrying a gun. It's about carrying information in your head at the same time.

What also started to bother me was that I was never able to find a gun review that wasn't sponsored by a firearms manufacturer. Every single gun review was completely positive, and the review would be on the left page and the full-page ad for the gun itself would be on the right. What a tip-off *that* was once I learned to look for it. The guns were always great, wonderful, flawless, and universally applicable to every situation.

A review should always be subjective, whether it's for a gun, a car, or a restaurant. That wasn't happening. I wanted reviews written by people who preferred polymer over steel (or vice-versa...just have an opinion on something!). I wanted to know if the factory sights were suitable or if it was better to opt for the tritium night sights. Is the slide release hard for small hands to reach? Does the pistol have a loaded chamber indicator? I wasn't finding any of that.

I became certain that there were tens of thousands of people in the United States who were going through the same process that I was and who shared my feelings. I read the blogs and letters to the editors of gun magazines; I was online all the time reading daily news articles. I sensed a real need, and a real concern, from people just like me.

It was around this time that there was a massive renewed interest in the concept of concealed carry. Yes, concealed carry had been around for years, but there were changes going on that were affecting people in different states. Periodically, the magazines on the market would run special editions or special articles on the topic, but then they'd go back to their same old editorials. Obviously, it worked for them. They didn't see any reason to change it.

It was another watershed moment for me. I never do anything halfway, and here was the opportunity I was looking for, just sitting there. There had to be other people out there like me who wanted to protect their families and who felt completely alone. They had to have the same questions I had—lots of them, in fact —and nowhere to find the answers.

This whole thing was far bigger than I could have ever expected. On one hand, it was about me and my family, but on the other hand, it was about other people's families. The full scale of how immense this could be was exciting and, to be honest, just a little frightening. But I could feel it calling to me. I had to do it.

"If it is to be, it's up to me." It had been true my whole life, and it had never been more clear than 30,000 feet above land in that moment on the airplane.

But I really did start the journey alone. The counterman at the store. The sheer lack of information out there. The fact that there was just *nothing* for someone like me who wanted to protect his family. All of these things...and yet, it was pretty simple and easy to wrap my head around. For someone who was used to engineering complexity into things, this was a revelation for me. It was so simple I couldn't believe it hadn't been done before. Why didn't this exist?

I was blazing a new trail, for sure.

CHAPTER 4

MY SECRET WEAPON

I joined the USCCA because you know what it means to be able to protect your family. Your teachings enable me to try to do it the right way. My family knows I will do everything possible to take care of them.

– Frank M., TX

I knew in the back of my head that Michigan Tech and its engineering program were going to be tough, but, man, did I have a lot of catching up to do. I remember looking out the window while in class and thinking, "My God...I don't know if I can do this." But when you want something, you find a way. You manage.

Michigan Tech is a blue-collar college. That's a compliment. It is a no-nonsense, straightforward, almost old-fashioned university with solid majors. It's also one of the least expensive universities in the Michigan educational system, which was good for me. Even better? I had managed to win several small scholarships in addition to the one I received at graduation.

Engineering was tough and included a lot of math, physics, chemistry, and related technical courses that required a strong academic foundation in order to jump right in. Even though I had good grades in high school, I received a heavy sucker punch when I took the math placement exam: I didn't place at the calculus level. Ouch. I didn't see that one coming at all. (It was an emotional setback, particularly since many of my friends *did* place in calculus and went on without me.) It meant I had to take additional math courses to get up to the calculus level, which in turn meant I started college behind the curve. I couldn't take many of the technical core classes I needed until I had taken calculus. Quite the Catch-22. I had to study all the time—it was still a heavy course load of difficult classes. It was truly up to me and only me —nobody gets you through courses like that except you. But I was determined to do it. My work ethic paid off in college, too.

I had to work a part-time job to make ends meet and, for that matter, be able to eat. Guess where I ended up working? Pizza Hut, the home of those three-times-a-year special Schmidt birthday dinners. I actually didn't mind it so much, because if you worked more than four hours on one shift you could make your own pizza and eat it. That saved me a lot of money...and really, what guy in college can't polish off an entire pizza on his own?

An engineering degree wasn't the only thing I was interested in at Michigan Tech. Now, you have to remember that, being an engineering school, girls were few and far between. But I somehow got lucky enough to live in a co-ed dorm and there was a girl on my floor. She was in my Introduction to Engineering Graphics course and she wore a mint green robe in the hallway. That's what I first remember about her.

It was Tonnie. And I was absolutely terrified to talk to her, which was out of character for me. (Sure, I was naturally shy, but I was okay talking to girls. They liked to talk to me.)

If you ask Tonnie, she has a bit of a different take on this:

> *So many girls were interested in Tim, but I wasn't. Girls made up about 10 percent of the student body and, well, they seemed to like him a lot. I wasn't rude to him*

or anything like that...I just wasn't interested. We had a class together, but it had more than 60 people in it, so he would go by in the stream of bodies. We'd chat a little bit on occasion...no big deal.

We also both lived in this super huge dorm—short, but with long hallways—and I always suspected he took the long way past my dorm room. There was this girl who lived kitty corner to me who had a huge crush on him; she was just gaga over him. It actually made me feel badly for him because she talked about him all the time. She acted so weird about it. Honestly? Chasing after some boy struck me as such an empty existence and waste of time, and I just didn't want anything to do with that.

Tim did come to my room once to ask me for help with some class—my door had been wide open—and he just stayed standing, which made me think he didn't need help at all, but I told him to do this and this and this...

Yeah, I didn't need help at all...but that didn't get me anywhere. She always seemed to have a boyfriend.

But then I ran into Tonnie at the end of sophomore year, and when I asked her if she had a boyfriend, she said "yes and no." I didn't know it at the time, but they were on the outs and she was trying to end it. We ended up having what she calls a "deep, philosophical, and drunk discussion" on her 19th birthday. I told her that if I could find a good woman, I would settle down, and she told me years later that at the time, she thought to herself, "I'm up for that. I'll marry you." It wasn't the most sober conversation in the world. She also couldn't say yes because she wasn't completely single, either.

But she ended up breaking up with her boyfriend, and we eventually started dating.

Tonnie was smart and worked hard throughout college, too. We studied together all the time, and I remember once while we were on the third floor of the library, I suddenly said to her, "If I came to you and said I wanted to start a business but had to risk everything, what would you say?" She looked at me for about two minutes, blinked once, and said, "I'd definitely do it." Just for the record, she has *always* been true to that attitude: in everything we've done and all the ventures we've tried, she's maintained an almost irrational belief in me. That belief—and her love for me—is just incredible, and it has really carried me through some tough times. I credit her for much of my personal and business development. Tonnie is no pushover either; she seriously saw something in me that nobody else did, even back then.

She actually graduated before I did due to her better math scores. We were in the same school year but a semester apart. We got married young. In fact, we returned to finish up college *after* we were married at Christmas during my fifth year of school. I was in the middle of my year and she was at the end of hers. Many people thought we were crazy to get married, but I wasn't about to let her slip away. Our wedding was small and modest: many newlyweds go off to Jamaica or Mexico or other more exotic places, but we went to Appleton, Wisconsin for three days and two nights. It was all we could afford, but we were in love and it was really the beginning of a beautiful life together. (Plus, we've always done what feels right for *us,* regardless of what other people *think* we should do.)

Graduating a semester before me meant that Tonnie entered the workforce first, and luckily she found a job in Massachusetts. It was 1994, and even in engineering, jobs were pretty thin. The economy wasn't the greatest back then. I was still in the co-op stage; I had actually snagged a "gig" with Kimberly-Clark. (When it came to a co-op, the idea was that it would eventually lead to a full-time job and then a career...contingent on performance, of course.) I needed a good job with a good company so that I could start paying my growing bills. With my successful stint at Kimberly Clark, I knew I would either be offered a job in Paris, Texas or Boston, Massachusetts.

With Tonnie in Massachusetts, I was really hoping for the Boston job to come through. Of course, it didn't. I was to be based in Paris, Texas. That wasn't going to work for us. Tonnie and I poured through the job ads and sent out many unsolicited resumes on the off chance someone was looking for a brand-new engineer just at the very moment my resume arrived in the mail. Those were rough statistical odds to be working with, but we kept trying.

Without an engineering job locked down, Tonnie and I decided to move to the East Coast. She had already taken a better job at that point on the "Big Dig," also known as the Central Artery/Tunnel Project. (Yep...she was already on her second job and I was unemployed. But it was a great step in her career as an engineer: the job was a rare opportunity to work on a one-of-a-kind construction project.)

We packed up everything we owned and headed off to a very small apartment in Natick, Massachusetts. It was all we could afford. Tonnie was earning the money that paid the bills, and I did the remodeling necessary for us to live there. I remember she had sent me to the hardware store to buy some very necessary fixtures for the bathroom. There I was, this big hayseed from Wisconsin, walking into the proverbial Yankee "mom-and-pop" hardware store. My typical Midwestern demeanor did nothing to impress the clerk, and I could barely understand his Bostonian accent. He asked me what I was smiling about. As you can imagine, it wasn't the best welcome to New England for me.

I kept sending out resumes without any luck. With the horrible economy, I needed *something,* so I took a job in a sporting goods store in Needham, Massachusetts stringing tennis racquets. I conveniently forgot to tell them two things: first, that I had never strung a tennis racquet before in my life, and second, that I had an engineering degree. (Apparently neither mattered, as I soon became an expert tennis racquet stringer!) I worked there for a solid seven months, stringing tennis racquets and mentally tallying up all the jobs on my resume that were *not* landing me the engineering job I'd hoped for: newspaper boy, grocery store clerk, cardboard box assembler, pizza server, and now tennis racquet stringer. I guess I could've added crayfish catcher, but that job didn't last long enough to be more than an occupational footnote.

Tonnie was just working crazy hours in Boston. And I kept sending out resumes, blasting the entirety of New England with them, just waiting for a call. It took six months, but I finally got a call and a job offer.

This came as a huge surprise to the sporting goods store management. In fact, when I finally went to them and told them that I was, in fact, an engineer and that I had been offered an engineering job, they told me that they'd been talking about me and really thought I was management material. I left on good terms, although I don't think they were particularly happy that I hadn't mentioned the whole engineer thing.

Like most young couples, Tonnie and I were open to new opportunities. We were both really trying to establish ourselves in our careers, but we were crazy enough to think we could take on more. And why not? We were young. We didn't have kids. We were supporting ourselves in our first real jobs.

And then friends of Tonnie's recruited us into a new venture that spring with a nationally-known, direct-selling, multi-level marketing company that offered a variety of consumer products. (Without mentioning it, you can figure out the company I'm talking about. Some people don't have very nice things to say about this company, or others like it, but I have to say it was one of the greatest things that ever happened to me. It taught me to look for the best in everyone.)

Initially, it appealed to me on so many levels. It satisfied my entrepreneurial streak; it was about being as successful as you wanted to be by putting in the effort. My success, our success, would be up to me—up to us. We were all in. The plan was that we would just be engineers until this took off and then we'd be our own bosses and be wildly successful at it.

We spent every dollar we could muster on that plan. We bought all the motivational tapes, all the books. And you know what? They were really, really good. I grew up listening to motivational tapes—to Tony Robbins and Zig Ziglar. So these were really no different. I owe a lot to those tapes and books and speakers because they really helped me to believe in myself: I could do whatever I set my mind to. It made me even more tenacious.

At the same time, we were really miserable. We didn't have a lot of money, and any money we did have went to attending monthly motivational talks and seminars in places like Poughkeepsie,

New York. It was all in addition to our regular jobs, so it also ate up our free time.

Yet, in five years, we never made a single cent on this "opportunity." In fact, it was just the opposite: we had *spent* almost $30,000. It was an incredibly powerful system, one that conditioned you into not quitting, into not giving up. There are winners and there are quitters in this world—which one are you going to be? Even after we did give it up, I still had regrets—I always thought that maybe the turning point would have been that next weekend or that next month. We could have done it. Sometimes I still think we could have done it. (That's how good multi-level marketing programs work: they make you believe you can absolutely succeed if you just hold on for a little more time.)

My day job was equally as interesting, but for very different reasons. It was my first professional engineering job, and it was at an awesome little company. We designed medical centrifuges. My direct boss was a former Israeli army captain, and he taught me a lot. He was *very* military—he could pick you apart and show you how you didn't know *anything*. My very first engineering drawing was a perfect example of that: it came back so marked up with red ink that I thought someone had bled to death on it. I could hardly read my underlying drawing, and I felt terrible. It crushed me—I'm a people pleaser and he clearly wasn't pleased. I had worked extra hard to produce what I felt was a very impressive first drawing. Wrong. (He did, however, tell me everything I did wrong in the nicest way that a former captain for the Israeli Defense Forces can.)

It was the kind of place that was very hands on, and I redeemed myself one very small step at a time. Eventually, I had the opportunity to be "all in" and really be a part of it. For a year, I had been doing three-dimensional computer modeling with some brand-new modeling software. (This was new technology for the mid-1990s, and it required special hardware and software to run it.) Since I was the new engineer on staff and just out of college, my computer skills were modestly good and probably better than the rest of the staff. The new setup still had bugs in it though, and I spent a lot of time communicating with the company that sold us the 3-D package. I developed a relationship very quickly with the entrepreneur who started the business...and we hit it off.

I wanted more. I quickly got the bug to make more money, achieve even more. I had been working hard for years at that point, first in college and then after graduation, and it wasn't exactly equating to wealth. I wasn't content with my first job or where Tonnie and I were in our lives, because I knew we weren't where we *could* be. Maybe a lot of people feel that way: that frustration when they are just starting out in their careers. Or maybe not. Maybe some people are perfectly content with that. I know I sure wasn't. I was restless. I wasn't necessarily motivated by greed, but I wanted to be in a place where the hard work I was doing was paying off in money, achievement, and satisfaction. I wasn't there yet.

That's when Shawn, the owner of the software company, approached me. "You're clearly the rock star here," he said. "You're a sharp guy. How would you like to make more money working for me selling this software, probably twice what you're making now?"

Wait a second. That was *exactly* what I was looking for. The timing couldn't have been more perfect. And so my response was essentially, "Dude, sign me up!"

It was really a perfect example of being in the right place at the right time. Engineering software was really hitting big then, and because I was an engineer by trade, I could become a sales engineer for the software company. I talked the talk—I could go in and speak with engineers and use their words and lingo and explain things to them—but I would also be involved in selling the software. Selling was a novel idea for me. It meant that I had to pick up the phone and cold call, and I was still quite shy. But it was easier than trying to sell something I had to learn about or pretend to believe in. I knew all about engineering and the software package itself. The selling part wasn't as bad as it could have been.

The owner of the company kept his existing territory—New England—and gave me everything else. It was good timing because Tonnie was still working on the Big Dig in Boston so she was really tied up with work. And me? Well, I was selling engineering software and hardware to the rest of the country.

Like my first job, I learned a lot from the owner. This time, my boss taught me a completely different lesson. He was an incredibly insecure man and not very likable. When he took off his software developer hat, he really wasn't much of anything. He was just a guy who had a good idea about some computer software, and he was able to get it up and running before the big guys got there and wrapped up the market. *That* was how he was a genius. Almost anything else he screwed up...even some of the simplest things. I observed him and what he did and his business model, and I thought, "Wow, if this guy can run a business like this and make a killing, *anyone* can." The problem was that Tonnie had just quit the Big Dig project due to the ridiculous hours she had to work and had started working for the same company. So it wasn't like we could both just bail at that point. Still, I could tell that Shawn was beginning to get a little nervous about me. I guess I can't blame him: I was bringing in a large percentage of company sales. Honestly, I think my knowledge also made him nervous.

Despite feeling a little bad about where I saw my and Tonnie's future with Shawn heading, I started putting together a plan. It wasn't a very good one, but it was a plan nonetheless. I wasn't going to go out and duplicate his business. First of all, it takes a lot of money to get into the "high-end" computer hardware business. I was definitely smart enough to realize that competing with him was a bad idea. It could have been a success, I guess, but it would have been an uphill battle. I also remembered what had happened to my dad when he started his own business back in Manitowoc, and I just didn't want to be that person who takes a guy's business from underneath him. As much as I didn't particularly care for Shawn, that just wasn't the right thing to do.

No, my plan was to take everything that was good about Shawn's business model and discard everything that was bad, and well, somehow come up with something that I could plug in and sell and make a profit. (So simple, yet about as clear as mud!) Honestly, I think anyone in my position would have done it. I had the perspective to see the holes, to see what he was doing well and what he was failing at. I also had the mind of an engineer—one that likes to iron out the problems. And his business had its fair share of those. (I later learned that it's hard to see your company's—and your own—flaws when you are a leader and a business owner. You can know there are problems, but be completely blind to them at the same time.)

So I didn't want to copy his exact business model, but I *did* know the engineering industry inside and out. Maybe I could come up with the *next* generation of software—it wouldn't necessarily put him out of business, right?—or some new, as-of-yet unknown software that would just revolutionize engineering. The possibilities were endless.

I was restless and I imagine I wasn't very good at covering my tracks at that point, so Shawn knew something was brewing. And he did what anyone in his position would have done when he found out: he fired me. I actually think he was looking for a reason to get rid of me, because it happened quickly: one day shortly after Tonnie and I had arrived to work, he fired both of us on the spot. We literally were escorted to the door with cardboard boxes full of our stuff.

I wasn't exactly sure what to do at that point. I was 23 years old and had just been fired from my job. And the "plan" I had brewing? Well, that wasn't ready just yet.

Tonnie and I didn't have anything else to do at that point, quite literally, so we decided to go to a movie. We were experiencing our first joint disaster. To her credit, Tonnie was handling it much better than I was.

We ended up in a movie theater seeing *Jerry Maguire*. And I sat in the movie theater and cried. I kept thinking, "I *am* Jerry Maguire." If you haven't seen that movie, go get it. You'll completely understand my mindset that afternoon.

Getting fired was one problem, but the bigger, more immediate problem was that Shawn fired me but still owed me a lot of money. I called my dad and he hooked me up with a really good attorney. I found out that Massachusetts has some of the most liberal, anti-business laws on the books in situations like these. If you take a business to court for withholding your commissions and they are found guilty, they owe you triple the damages. Oh, dang!

I went in there and demanded that Shawn pay me what he owed me, and it didn't take too much persuasion for that to happen. He clearly didn't want to risk going to court, knowing that he was obligated to pay me and that it could definitely end up costing him far more than he actually owed. It was a very smart move on his part.

I wasn't exactly sure what my next move would be, but it clearly involved Tonnie. We kept going back to what my parents had drilled into me from childhood on: that it was important to be near family. Tonnie was from Michigan and I was from Wisconsin, so we took a serious look at Milwaukee.

Milwaukee was founded on manufacturing, and even though it's not the manufacturing center it once was, it was still full of opportunity for two engineers like us. We had enough experience under our belts that we weren't green anymore. We were credible, experienced engineers—why not create a small engineering firm? (After graduating from tennis racquet stringing and moving into the engineering world, I figured I had enough experience to branch out on my own. I knew what I wanted to do and what I didn't want to do and thought, heck, I can do this. I can start my own business.) Milwaukee seemed like a perfect place to try that idea out. That was the missing piece to my plan. Shawn really had nothing to worry about. I wasn't going to sell engineering software after all. I was going to sell my engineering *talent* to Milwaukee manufacturers: Harley-Davidson, Master Lock, Milwaukee Tool... maybe even Allen-Bradley.

So we packed up everything in a U-Haul and headed to Milwaukee. Tonnie went to stay with my parents in Manitowoc and I slept in a buddy's guest bedroom for three months while I tried to figure out our next best move in establishing Schmidt Engineering.

I ended up taking a contract position with Milwaukee Forge, a forging and heat treating company on Milwaukee's south side. (A lot of engineers work as contractors in the industry. It's an arrangement that can work well for some people. It wasn't exactly what I wanted to be doing, but I'm not knocking it by any means.) I continued to put out feelers, though, to see what else was out there.

I stumbled upon an ad that listed a consulting opportunity in a western Milwaukee suburb. It was very vague: it simply said "consultant." But that one word told me all I needed to know. It was for a small consulting firm—essentially, the very same idea I had—with about 10 engineers, working for some of the companies that I wanted to work for, like John Deere. That's not a Milwaukee business, but it's based in Moline, Illinois, which is not too far away. Plus they have plants all over and a lot of the Milwaukee manufacturers supply them with parts. John Deere would be a great addition to my resume, if I could get it.

The more I thought about it, the more I realized this little firm was *exactly* the business I wanted to create. I figured to get in there wasn't a bad idea at all. First, it was a job, and second, I could pick up what I needed to learn about business. The engineering side I had down, but I needed to learn more.

I left my contract position, which wasn't a big deal. Contracts have an end date anyway...typically when the project is over and they don't need you anymore. I started working as a consultant, and while it was a good job, I wasn't making any progress on Schmidt Engineering, which was frustrating. I couldn't go into the consulting firm during the day to work on my side projects, because the company was fully staffed and all the computers were in use. And there was no way I could afford my own license; it was incredibly expensive.

One of the owners offered a novel solution: he could lease us the use of his licenses at night, when nobody was around. It was perfectly legal—it's called "floating the license"—and it meant that Schmidt Engineering work could be done from 7 p.m. until 7 a.m. There was enough engineering business to go around, so floating us that license wouldn't really compete with his business and he would bring in a little extra cash. It was a good opportunity all around, and really was the missing piece in my business plan. I had started with the best and worst of Shawn, found what I could do to actually make money, secured a license, and there you go… we were able to make Schmidt Engineering a legitimate business.

I started cold calling every manufacturing company in the Milwaukee area with a possible need for engineering services— a job I absolutely hated. It was tough to be out there calling and getting rejected day after day. That kind of thing really takes its toll on you. To this day, if there's one thing I really hate, it's being rejected.

Schmidt Engineering did manage to snag a gig a little further south: we did a lot of work during a three-month period for a company in Racine, which is about a half hour from Milwaukee. It was our first real client, and it turned out to be a complete disaster. The work assignment had a critical deadline and, since this was a brand-new client, I overpromised. I really wanted to please and impress, but he certainly didn't care about reciprocating. When it came to paying me, he told me he had to wait until he was paid by the subcontractor he was working for, who claimed he had to be paid by the contractor…and so on. I must've been about five rungs down the payment ladder.

I bought it though, and the guy ended up owing me more than $30,000, which he never did pay me. I was really contemplating ending Schmidt Engineering. It just wasn't happening and it was an incredibly hard schedule for me to keep up working those hours.

I had taken a break to visit a friend in Chicago and was driving home. My pager went off with a number to call back. Remember pagers? Back then, I couldn't even afford a cell phone, so I had to pull off at the rest stop and use the payphone to call the number back. (Try finding a payphone now, or even explaining the concept of one to your kids or grandkids.)

It was a call from Mayville Engineering, one of the hundreds of companies I'd cold called without any success. They'd kept my information and had a big project that they needed help with— one that could possibly last two or three years.

It was the break we needed. However, it also created new problems. Up until that point, I was able to get around the fact that Schmidt Engineering never had a physical office by conveniently offering to meet our clients at *their* workplaces. You know how it goes: "Well, I just happen to have another appointment out by you that day, so I can stop by…" I had mastered the workaround by that point.

But that just wasn't going to fly anymore. This was a company that wanted and needed to come to us once in a while, and while I was able to stretch it another two, three months, we definitely were at a point where we needed physical space. We ended up renting an office for $600 a month, and then we hired one person. And then another one.

I'll be the first to admit that my leadership and management skills were non-existent back then. It showed, and I needed extra help in that area. I never had any trouble working as an engineer. I could focus and just get stuff done. But that skill set didn't include Tim the Manager.

Still, we established a real, legitimate engineering company, with employees and an actual office. We were able to establish a name for ourselves, and pretty soon we were getting jobs by word of mouth. Schmidt Engineering expanded to four engineers. But I did a lot of hiring and firing during that time, too. Throughout that time period, I was able to find some really good engineers, which was a smart move on my part. I hired people who were better than I was.

We also developed a reputation of always exceeding expectations. We were an expensive engineering firm—we were never the lowball quote—but we gave our clients what they paid for without exception. They knew if they came to us, they would pay more and the job would be done well.

Now, I'd love to say that Schmidt Engineering was a success. It never made a ton of money, but it definitely made enough to support my family. I was really willing to do anything to make it work, but in the process I really abused myself. It was a really hard way to make a living the way we were going about it. It was either super busy or super slow, and I worked so many nights. Tonnie and I had started a family, and it was hard on her.

It became really clear that I needed a Plan B. I've never been a content person. When I look back, that's so clear to me. I wasn't content in that first real job in Boston, and here I was, a business owner, and I still wasn't completely happy. And I was really no longer content in having an *engineering* business. I needed a product I could sell. I needed something with more leverage.

I came up with a whole line of home security products. I even had a name for it: Schmidt Tactical. But I had no marketing plan at all... just product development. Scratch that idea.

Then I had an idea for a modular garage door system. And honestly, it was a darn good idea. But again, it was all about the product development. I had no idea how I could ever sell it. Scratch that idea, as well.

I soon figured out that the only way to make a business work in the long term is to have awesome marketing, too. You can have the world's worst product, and believe me, there's a lot of stuff out there that's been developed that's just terrible and useless, yet consumers think they need it, and that's because the product has awesome marketing. That was my problem: I didn't have awesome marketing. I really didn't have any marketing sense at all.

That was about 2003, and I started to sense that I needed to do something else. I had always bought gun magazines off and on, and had never really lost the good memories I had growing up with my dad. Tim Jr. had been born, and I had that moment on the airplane: *If it is to be, it's up to me.*

I was so listless and my discontent had grown to the point where something had to change. I had my concealed carry idea, and it was becoming more appealing every day. But people thought I was crazy when I mentioned it. I had what looked like a successful business, and I should have been on top of the world. Why would I want to give all that up? It just made no sense to anyone except me—and Tonnie, who just unconditionally supported me all along.

It was time for me to channel all that frustration and listlessness into something. I had to somehow move from just having all these great ideas to actually turning them into a real, concrete plan— one that made sense for our future. I could sit and dream about what I could do for the rest of my life...or I could go out there and get started.

CHAPTER 5

ENGINEERS, MAGAZINES & STRUGGLES

*I first joined USCCA for the knowledge base. I felt the enormous
responsibility I was undertaking when carrying a weapon. My wife
and I talked this over and after some more serious discussions, we
decided. We thought maybe these guys would be the best way for
us to move forward. I wanted someone I could trust.
So we took the chance.*

– William B., TN

I would be lying if I didn't say I was burned out on Schmidt Engineering at that point. It was clear that my mind was elsewhere with all the self-defense ideas I was generating. It wasn't fair to anyone: to Schmidt Engineering, to our employees, to Tonnie, or even to me.

But the idea of a magazine...now that was something. The best part was that there wasn't a magazine out there like I envisioned. It was pretty simple: start a magazine for people who are interested in protecting their families.

The first thing I did was run out and buy three books on how to start a magazine. And then, to be honest, I didn't read them. Thank God. It's the best thing I never did. Instead, I put the hammer down and methodically figured out how to do it myself, step by step. I put an ad on Craigslist to hire someone to teach me the basics of how to lay out a magazine. A guy came to Schmidt Engineering, which I still owned, and spent 12 hours giving me a crash course on how to do it.

The first issue, if you have it, is really not so pretty. On somewhat of a fluke, the model on the cover eventually became the magazine's art director. My picture is on page one as another model. I'm all over page 21, illustrating the "quick draw ability" of a concealed carry holster. Gun reviewer Fred W. Black? Yep, that's me too.

Most of the magazine was in black and white, with blue spot color. It was printed on low-quality paper. It's a far cry from the glossy four-color magazine we do today. But it was a good start, and nobody realized it was essentially put together by one person.

I ultimately did the entire first issue of *Concealed Carry Magazine* from start to finish by myself. I took the photos, wrote the articles, laid it out, and bought a mailing list of 30,000 names and addresses (which, to be honest, also required an incredible investment in postage). Honestly, it was money we really didn't have to spend, but what other choice did I have?

I knew absolutely nothing about the strategy behind selling a magazine and why publishers do the things that they do, but I somehow decided on a false cover to help promote the magazine.

In keeping with that, I also devised a strategy to get subscribers: the first 500 people who subscribed would receive a solid brass .45 ACP keychain. Even better, those first subscribers would be entered to win an actual gun!

And then there was the most brilliant thing I did, which was really more of an afterthought: on the front cover, I noted that this brand-new magazine was the official publication of the United States Concealed Carry Association (which technically didn't even exist yet!). I figured that when I had time, I'd get around to setting that up, but for then, it gave the magazine some credibility. It looked good, too.

It took me around five months to lay out the entire magazine, which is an eternity in the publishing world. I could barely afford the mailing costs—not to mention printing. But I had done everything by myself, which meant I had no labor costs, either. The learning curve just never seemed to end, nor did the cost. I pulled all the equity out of my house and put it on the line.

I wrapped it up, sent it out to those 30,000 addresses, and crossed my fingers.

My first vision was that the mail truck was going to roll up in a few days with just bags and bags of subscriptions. That never happened, and it still hasn't happened. But I have always worn rose-colored glasses—I always think "this is the one." Optimism is something you are either born with or you aren't. We all have the capacity to develop it. But people like me are born with it. And that's why we keep plugging away at things when other people quit.

The mail truck and the bags of responses never arrived. What *did* I get? An initial three-percent response rate, which meant something both terrible and promising.

The good news? I actually had subscribers. And that meant I had to do more issues. The bad news? With an initial plan of six issues annually, at the current rate I was going, it would take me two and a half years to put out an entire year of the magazine!

The initial feedback was mostly good, though. It reinforced my suspicion that there were many people out there just like me. Here's a sampling of the feedback we received from that first issue:

> *"I was very impressed upon looking over and reading the free sample of* Concealed Carry Magazine. *I could really relate. Your magazine has a bright future."*
> —Alex, New York

> *"I enjoyed your free issue. I am always willing to learn more."*
> —Tom, Alabama

> *"I received your introductory issue of* Concealed Carry Magazine *and found it to be a very refreshing change from ordinary gun magazines."*
> —LeRoy, Texas

> *"Congratulations on a great magazine!"*
> —David, Florida

> *"I enjoyed your magazine very much…I am looking forward to the next issue."*
> —Marilyn, Michigan

> *"I find your no-nonsense, real-world focus to be a refreshing change from other gun publications."*
> —Keith, Ohio

> *"I very much enjoy reading your magazine. I especially like the article that gives me ammunition to argue successfully for our Second Amendment rights."*
> —Todd, Minnesota

"I just wanted to write and express how much I enjoyed the article, 'Constitutional Right and Social Obligation to Carry.'"
—Matt, Washington

"I hope each issue does not appear to be one giant advertisement for Glock."
—Gary, Oregon

Our first issue had only one gun review and it was for Glock. Sorry, Gary.

But the rest of the feedback, which amounted to hundreds of messages, affirmed that I was on the right track. And nobody just flat-out said it was terrible, which was also a good sign. Gosh, it just felt great.

It soon became clear that with just that first issue, I had hit a completely untapped market. Over the course of the next few months, about 100 people emailed me, asking if they could write for the magazine. (The magazine looked good, or at least good enough for those first few issues!) Some of the easier parts were falling into place right away.

But I was doing the magazine stuff at night and around my regular engineering work that was still going on at Schmidt Engineering. And so I panicked and scrambled, putting out an ad for an actual, honest-to-God editor. Maria became the very first employee at Delta Defense.

And there were other problems. I had no sense of scale, of the actual expense of printing a magazine on an offset press. I can sum that up in one word: expensive.

I also didn't have any advertisers, and I was dead set against the traditional business model of using advertising to fund the magazine. I wanted subscribers to fund it...not advertisers. In the magazine world, advertisers spend a lot of money to get their product advertisements in front of readers. Those ads also lend credibility to the readers; if you have the big guns (no pun intended) advertising in your magazine, then you must be legitimate. But I didn't want the influence of advertisers. I wanted to be able to write product reviews that were real and that told the readers the good and the bad without worrying about ticking anybody off.

Honestly, it was a huge pain. Without relying on advertising—and without gaining more subscribers—it was hard to move forward. I was really struggling financially and with getting things rolling. The magazine was far from successful; it was slowly chugging to life.

But after we put out more issues, more parts started to fall into place. We didn't have any great exodus of those original subscribers, which was a good sign. There was a lot to write about—the magazine was in no danger of becoming stale anytime in the near future.

The main struggle was money. I had taken the traditional publishing model and turned it completely upside down. But that also came at a cost. In about nine months, I had managed to burn through $115,000. The magazine was hemorrhaging cash. Salaries, overhead, publishing, printing, and mailing all cost a ton of money—a lot more than subscription receipts were bringing in.

The financial side of the publishing business was where my complete lack of experience was becoming a big problem. I felt like a rat in one of those wheels that just keeps spinning. I couldn't get advertisers because I didn't have that many subscribers yet.

(Advertisers want circulation numbers to justify their advertising expense.) On top of that, I didn't really want advertisers in the first place, but I finally had to admit that I needed them to pay for the magazine. If I tried to find outside investors, what would they look at? Among other things, they'd want to know who was advertising in the magazine. It was a point I had to bend on. Even though our subscriber base was growing, I was still directly competing against other well-established gun magazines. I needed to figure out a way to raise more money, reposition myself, or preferably both.

HERE'S MY CLASSIC MAGAZINE PUBLISHER JOKE

Q: *Hey, do you know the fastest way to get to a million bucks?*

A: *Easy. Start with two million and then build a magazine from scratch!*

I can laugh about it now, but at the time, the reality of that joke was all too true. Sure, I had started a new magazine and had even managed to get a few subscribers, but I nearly broke the bank doing it.

For the time being, Schmidt Engineering essentially became the magazine's sugar daddy; *Concealed Carry Magazine* became "Tim's super expensive hobby." I was devoting more and more of my time to the magazine, to getting the next issue out, and less time to the business. From 2004 until halfway through 2005, that's how I worked. It was all about getting through the next month, then the next month, and the magazine just needed more and more money.

The employees at Schmidt Engineering were basically working around me and leaving me alone (and vice versa). It wasn't an optimum situation by any means. While they spent their time engineering, I spent my time either on the phone or packing up boxes of magazines. I'm not kidding you. I would put the boxes together and then put extra copies of the magazine inside them and mail them out. I had come up with this idea that people could choose from just a subscription or—an even better deal— they could also pay for the back issues that they'd missed and I'd send them out. It helped me get rid of the excess copies, but it also took up a lot of my time.

In my personal life, things weren't much easier. We had built a house; we'd been there a year and we still hadn't poured our driveway. With all the bills I had with the magazine and in keeping Schmidt Engineering afloat, taking care of our driveway was very low on the priority list. I was essentially working two full-time jobs and things were still financially a mess. I couldn't really afford to feed my family and the magazine at the same time.

One night, I just couldn't sleep because things were weighing so heavily on me, and I went outside around 11:30 p.m. I was sitting there, stressed out of my mind with my feet in the gravel. I remember telling myself, "You either gotta figure this out or pull the plug." Tonnie was asleep, and our family had grown to include three children at this point: Tim Jr., Dagny, and Sten. I was scared. I didn't know what to do. I was more than $100,000 in debt and on the verge of bankruptcy. I was working as hard as I could, and it wasn't enough. I had hit my own personal line in the sand where I needed to decide whether or not to call it quits. It was honestly one of the lowest moments of my life.

I decided I needed investors to keep things afloat. By this time, we were living in West Bend and I had gotten to know some of the bigwigs in town, and so I started there. Being an engineer, I wrote up a detailed plan, which engineers are very good at doing. I sent out about 100 of them with self-addressed, stamped envelopes. I got 25 of them back—all basically rejection letters. Half of those said they didn't believe in the idea; the others just said no. The rest just didn't respond at all. I was deflated, sure, but I was mostly angry. I knew it was a good idea, and it didn't really make any sense to me that no one else could see that. To this day, I still remember who those people are. I see some of them all the time.

Out of all those packets I sent out, I did get *one* positive response. There was someone who was willing to back my idea. I had sent one to my dad, just to show him what I was doing. He responded that he would back me. He was the only one. The fact that he did that meant more to me than any financial backing could have. I didn't take his money, but the fact that he believed in me just reinforced the idea that I was on to something important. It made me realize that I would figure out a way to make it happen. It meant so much to me that my dad was willing to invest in my business idea. It still does. In fact, I still get choked up when I think about it. That was such an important thing he did for me. He knew if it was to be, it was up to me, but that didn't mean he couldn't support me like he had always done. He was willing to make a real investment in me and my idea.

Looking back on things now, I'm sure a lot of people didn't understand why I wanted to bail on a successful business—especially an engineering business: the epitome of stability.

(The only business that has to look more stable to outsiders is accounting. And that's not to knock either of them. How many times do you hear of these kinds of businesses being in trouble? You just don't.) Schmidt Engineering did look successful, and it was—to a certain degree.

But it just wasn't a business I had any interest in anymore. That's not really something that people can see—nor can you express that discontent to people, particularly if you own the business. It's not something you bring up over cocktails at your favorite restaurant or at a cookout with your neighbors. You can't just say, "Hey, this isn't doing it for me anymore." People look at you strangely when you make statements like that.

Around this time, I also started studying marketing. It was as if the missing piece fell into place for me. I had all these great ideas—and some not so great ones—but I just didn't know how to market them. Same with the magazine. We were marketing it by placing these little ads in other magazines. It was so expensive, but it was working. Subscribers were trickling in. But there had to be a better way.

Still, I was prepared to work, and work hard, to make it succeed. I'm the ultimate eternal optimist. I can think a glass is half full… even if there's only one drop in it. I was teaching myself marketing and darn it, I needed to try some of that stuff.

Nothing was easy about those first few attempts to market the magazine. I remember I packed up a bunch of issues and went off to the SHOT Show. I couldn't afford to actually have a booth at the show, so I figured I would do the next best thing: I'd walk in, walk around, talk to people, hand out copies of the magazine, and maybe get a few subscriptions. I didn't know it at the time, but it turns out that trade show organizers, as well as other exhibitors, absolutely hate it when people do this. Unfortunately, it wasn't the opportunity I thought it would be. I really thought it was going to be the big break that the magazine needed—that people would be lining up to talk to me.

In fact, it was the exact opposite. I'd walk up to people with the magazine and introduce myself: "Hi, I'm Tim Schmidt and I'm the publisher of *Concealed Carry Magazine!*" Now, imagine how hard that was for me. That's not something that comes naturally to me at all.

Most of the people I approached would just look at me and walk away without even taking a copy. A few accepted copies just to be polite, but those copies probably went right into the show garbage cans. That was not how I thought it would go. At all. But I kept trying. The really sad thing was that when all was said and done, I came home with just about as many magazines as I had left with.

BOB BROWN LEARNS OF
THE MAGAZINE

One important thing did happen at that first SHOT Show. I was able to meet Bob Brown, publisher of Soldier of Fortune *magazine. He kind of looked me up and down and said, "So this is your magazine." He paged through it and told me exactly what he thought.*

"It's not a very good idea. It's never going to work."

Now, after going through what I did with getting Concealed Carry Magazine *off the ground, I had developed a profound respect for anyone in the publishing business. Creating and maintaining a magazine is hard work. And here was this guy, the founder/editor/publisher of a magazine that I had bought, telling me that my idea was no good. Ouch.*

That wasn't exactly what I had been hoping to hear. At the very least, I hoped he'd have said something nice as a sort of professional courtesy. But it wasn't the first time someone had told me I'd fail. And so I respectfully went on my way, fueled by his criticism.

I did have a moment of sweet justice about a year ago. I'm not sure if Bob's personal opinion of Concealed Carry Magazine *had changed or not—and it really doesn't matter either way—but I found out that we got a call from* Soldier of Fortune. *They wanted to know if we would trade advertising space with them. I'd like to think that by reaching out to us, they respect what we're doing. I respect their magazine. Always have.*

The thing is, *Concealed Carry Magazine* has always been a little different than everything else on the market. Remember when I slapped the USCCA logo on the front? Once I actually got the association established, the magazine really became a member benefit. You couldn't just subscribe to the magazine; you got it when you became a member.

Of course, now you can just subscribe without joining the USCCA, but the people who do that are in the minority. We offer this option primarily so they can get a taste of what the USCCA is about and what it does, with the hopes that they will come on board with us. But if they don't, that's okay too. Hopefully someday they'll change their minds.

It's an expensive undertaking to produce a magazine. You have people on staff, the writers, the printing costs, and the postage, which just keeps getting more expensive.

Regardless of how you look at it, though, *Concealed Carry Magazine* has evolved into a great publication. See, most magazines are for-profit ventures. When you go to the bookstore or newsstand and pick up a magazine, the size of it is completely dependent on how many ads it sells in a particular month. If it's a bad month, the magazine will be thinner. A great month? A nice, fat issue. They rely on ad sales to print that magazine.

Not us. *Concealed Carry Magazine* is not reliant on ads. Sure, we happily accept advertisers (and we're thankful for them), but we're publishing a magazine for responsibly armed Americans...not for gun manufacturers. We're not in the magazine business. We're in the business of providing top-notch education and training for our readers. I guess when we first started, that idea probably did sound a little weird. It's very different, and it's still different.

We also got a little more clarity in 2005 when I "officially" created the United States Concealed Carry Association. It had been in the planning stages for more than a year—really, it went from a last minute decision to slap it on the front of the magazine to an actual, real-life entity—and as the magazine progressed, I was able to refine an actual concept for what the association could be and what role the magazine would play as a member benefit. Of all the moving parts that have comprised the USCCA, the magazine has really stayed consistent.

Really, it comes down to this: our magazine is not about guns. The focus is on the responsible *people* who own guns.

To tell you the truth, I really enjoy reading *Concealed Carry Magazine*. That sounds kind of funny, but the association has grown to the point where I'm not as involved as I was at the beginning… and that's an extremely good thing. There's a great team in place that brings the magazine to life now. I still write a short message for each issue, but most of what you see is because we have some of the best people in the industry working their tails off.

Looking back, the realization that I needed some serious marketing intervention really was a turning point for the magazine. I had gotten to the point where I could recognize that there was this gigantic hole and I had no idea how to fill it. Like everything else I'd hit up until that point, I knew it was something I could learn. Someone could teach me how to do it. The question was, who?

I ended up stumbling across Yanik Silver, the author and serial entrepreneur. Yanik is the founder of the Underground Online seminars. He was holding a conference in Washington, D.C. that focused on direct response marketing on the internet. I knew that was something that could really take the magazine and everything I envisioned about the magazine to the next level. It was perfect timing too—direct response marketing had been around for years, but the internet took it to a whole new level.

I had to go.

It was $750 plus airfare to get there and back—which was a good chunk of money that we really needed to finish our driveway. (That's how difficult things had become financially. We didn't even have the money to pour a driveway and there I was, contemplating going to this seminar.)

But yeah...I really had to go. And I wasn't going to tell Tonnie. It wasn't that I was hiding it from her, but that was just the way she had become conditioned to dealing with our financial issues: it was better not to know the details. I found a credit card that had some room on it and booked the seminar.

I went. I was sitting at the seminar and listening to speaker after speaker, and thinking, "This is just crazy, absolutely crazy." These speakers...they were on to something. They were making sense. It was like I had been the blind man and now I could see.

Then Yanik got up. He said he'd thought long and hard about something and he wasn't really interested in doing it, but he thought there were some people who could really benefit from something called "high-level maintenance"—his Mastermind Series—for the upcoming year. He was only going to offer it to a certain number of people, and then he was going to cap it. And it would cost $10,000 for the year...even more money we didn't have. (If I actually did have that $10,000, there was a huge list of things that it should have been spent on first before this series.)

But I felt something stir inside me—and I knew I had to go.

I took an application, went back to the hotel room, and filled it out. This application was huge—something like 13 or 15 pages. I knew this was my opportunity. I stayed up for hours and then when I returned to the seminar the next morning, I went up to Yanik and introduced myself.

The good news arrived shortly thereafter: I was accepted into the program. We didn't have the money, and it really was a crazy, impulsive decision on my part, but it honestly ranks up there as one of the best decisions I've made in my life. I would find the money somewhere.

I went to the first meeting and those people—those original attendees—became some of my best business friends. They were brilliant, brilliant people. One guy had sold his business the year before for $10 million. If they weren't people who could help you, they knew people who knew the guy who could.

We met that first year and everyone got an hour. We talked about what we were working on and what we needed help with. It was the ultimate in accountability—we were all in the same boat together, trying to succeed and help each other at the same time.

We were able to quickly identify real problems and offer real solutions. What was so awesome was that we were all doing different things, in different parts of the country, so our knowledge base was huge. We were naturally accountable—we felt an obligation to each other, we had similar personality types, and we'd all invested $10,000 in the series (but really, it was an investment in ourselves and our businesses)—and had such a high level of effective execution after talking to each other. We could take those problems and come up with solutions and turn things around so quickly.

During that time, I decided that it was time to let Schmidt Engineering go. I wasn't doing the company or the employees any favors, because my heart clearly wasn't in it at all. By 2006,

I'd fully come out of the proverbial closet at work. I was doing far more concealed carry work in the office; the guys could see the writing on the wall.

But throughout my time as a business owner, I had learned a few good things. For example, I'd hired two particular engineers named Bob and Brian who were far better engineers than I was. (Good business owners should always hire people who are better than them in what they do.) Bob and Brian weren't just good engineers, either. They were good people who were committed to Schmidt Engineering, even if I wasn't. (I did have one employee who quit in the middle of a project and headed off into the sunset —he even left the state!—because he was so mad at me. I had to step in and fix that mess, which Bob helped me with. Eventually I was able to mend fences with that employee and, to be honest, I don't blame him for what he did.)

Bob ended up buying Schmidt Engineering from me, and it still exists. He changed the name but still keeps the tie to Schmidt Engineering, as he's still working with some of our original clients and that's how they first knew him. It's okay though. It makes me happy to see that it's still going and it's essentially turned into the kind of place I'd hoped it would be. Schmidt Engineering was a good idea; it just wasn't a good idea for me. I'm happy that Bob enjoys that success now.

The point at which I'd walked away from engineering and fully into concealed carry was interesting. I was working at Delta Defense, full time. I was actually making money at it. I was hiring people, real employees, and building a new business.

I'd been part of the Mastermind series for about four years at that point, and it had helped me tremendously. But I was at an inflection point. I'd outgrown the series. It wasn't as beneficial as it once was. I needed to do something else. I started to work with a mentor, Robert Hirsch.

That year, I spent about half my time wanting to hug him and the other half wanting to kill him. I'd fly in to meet him and he would just sit down and wing it. No preparation, no formal outline or anything. Honestly, in our meetings, he did very little talking at all. The focus was all on me.

I thought I was going to sit down and he was going to give me some kind of engineering formula, but for marketing. Wrong. I was so wrong about that. I thought it was going to be nuts and bolts stuff. But all he wanted me to do was work on the intangible things about being an owner and a leader. I kinda sucked it up at that point and just did it. I was paying for it, after all. But I do have to admit: in one year, he taught me what I was missing. Delta Defense was able to go from 10 to 35 employees.

So what was his secret sauce? It was about teaching me emotional intelligence—even basic leadership. He taught me that it was okay to be vulnerable. He showed me how I avoided confrontation and I wasn't able to set clear expectations for my employees, which made their jobs difficult. Really, it was basic, basic leadership stuff. Stuff I was missing. By learning that side of things, though —the emotional side—he took me much further than I ever could have gone on my own.

Still, his technique just drove me nuts. See...one thing I have always been able to do is to recognize when I'm not good at something. And the second is that I have the ability to seek out people who are good at that something: people who can either help me or do it for me. But I don't like it when people operate the way Robert did.

I was paying him for his time, and I felt he should have somehow prepared for our meetings. But he seemed to just wing it every time. (Maybe he did prepare, but he didn't prepare the way I prepare for things. I didn't see any notes or an outline or structure at all, really.) I know I said it before, but he really did drive me nuts. At the same time, he was the best advisor I could have had at that point.

See...I was already good at believing in myself. But Robert Hirsch taught me the importance of getting *other* people to believe in me.

And then there were the lessons I'd learned throughout my career up to that point. I remembered Shawn, the owner of the software company who recruited me away from my first engineering job. I had decided if I ever started my own business, I'd be just the opposite of him. He never trusted anyone, and he had told me to never trust anyone. He was my own personal honey badger.

I carried the unconditional support I had from Tonnie. She believed in me when she probably shouldn't have. You don't know how profound that is until you have it. You can struggle so much with a partner who doesn't do that, and yet everything I came up with to that point...well, she was there 100 percent, no matter how outlandish it was. That's what got me through—if she believed in me, then I knew I could succeed. The power of that belief is incredible.

And I am a huge risk taker. Huge. But I only take risks that I understand. And when I understand them, I go 110 percent. Why? Just because, I guess. It's my personality. I truly live life by "If it is to be, it's up to me."

I think that's why I've always been attracted to the kind of things I've done. None of them were mistakes—even the huge investment we made trying to be independent contractors with the consumer products company. It was a good investment because it really affirmed the power of believing in yourself. I walked away from that with a lot of good training. It was just a matter of finding that million-dollar idea and executing what I'd learned. A million dollar idea executed well has incredible returns. Heck, even a ten-dollar idea with brilliant execution can do the same thing.

CHAPTER 6

MISTAKES & BREAKTHROUGHS

I joined the USCCA because I wanted the latest information from others who also believed in protecting themselves, their friends, and their families. I am always willing to share with others what I know and have learned as well as where I get my information.

– Matthew S., MO

I certainly made plenty of mistakes on my journey. Boy, did I make a lot of them. But the best motivation happens when you back yourself into a corner. That's when you work like heck to get out.

The first mistake was internal, and members didn't know about it.

See, as *Concealed Carry Magazine* grew and evolved into the actual United States Concealed Carry Association, so did the company behind it. (I was smart enough to realize that Tim Schmidt Inc., which was four employees, was not scalable. And that was a good thing!) By 2011, we were up to 10 employees. But then we exploded; we added 15 more people to the team in just a few short months.

Of the 15 new hires, though, 12 were mistakes.

The problem? I had hired mostly friends and a few acquaintances who needed jobs. I didn't really have any sort of system in place at that time, and I was mostly hiring people just based on instinct—which turned out to be a gigantic mistake.

Half of the people I had brought on board should have never been hired in the first place, and the other half was set up to fail. I was still quite poor at defining direction and pretty unsupportive as a boss. I had also hired quite a few people with the expectation that they would be like me: ultra driven and relentless when it came to execution. Of course, that sort of thing rarely works out.

We had a few really bad apples in that group of 15, and it wasn't just about their work performance. They brought down the whole organization. Existing B players on the team started to be C players. Even the A players weren't delivering like usual.

Honestly, things were just a mess. It didn't help that we were continuing to grow amidst all the internal turmoil. I was constantly having to reassure people about the situation. And eventually, I had to step up and make some really hard decisions.

It was a horrible position to be in, but I had to let some of those bad apples go. Inevitably, that included a few friends, some of whom I haven't seen or talked to since. (I did run into one guy a few times, and though we made small talk, it was strained and awkward.)

But those changes were ones that had to be made. And I had to be the one to make them.

Looking back now, the whole thing reminds me of ripping off a Band-Aid. Do you do it in one quick tug and get it over with or do you just keep endlessly peeling it off? Which hurts more?

As painful as that experience was, it needed to happen. Within six months, we were back down to about 12 employees, and things started to turn around pretty quickly.

It was around that time that I moved on to a new strategic coach. I was now working with Duane Marshall, who helped me immensely. He taught me what I needed to know at that point: how to create and implement systems. People didn't have to be just like me for us to succeed: they just had to be able to *understand* me.

That had been a problem. The engineer in me would surface and I would come up with some complex idea or system and complicate it to the point where it made sense to me but absolutely no sense at all to anyone else. When you make something overly complex, you run the risk of nobody understanding it. And that doesn't work.

I credit Duane for pulling me back on that, for showing me that maybe that wasn't the best way to do it. He taught me that if you can be a good, clear leader, you can lead ordinary people to do extraordinary things. That made sense to me.

I also worked, and continue to work, with Dan Sullivan, who is based in Toronto. It's funny—he works with a bunch of people and we all get together every quarter, kind of like a class. It's about 25 of us from all over the place, and we represent every single type of business possible. It's interesting, because when you get down to it, we all have the same exact problems. I've never been afraid to ask for help; you need that input if you want to reach your goals. And there is some comfort in knowing that other people are in the same exact boat you are.

If Duane was the A-10 watching from 10,000 feet to strafe tanks, Dan was the stealth bomber at 50,000 feet pushing buttons and blowing stuff up. You need people like that to help you. I'd never be where I am today without their guidance over the years.

Sometimes you, as a leader, have to hold your nose and take some big jumps to move forward. If you're at that point in a decision that has the potential to really make or break your business, you better hope you've done a lot of soul searching about what you're about to do. You can make that decision based on raw guts and instinct or you can do the proverbial "big picture" thinking. You can also sit and navel gaze, but that rarely gets you anywhere. I'm not the kind of guy who can do that for very long without getting restless. I'd rather make some mistakes along the way than just sit and worry about whether or not something will work out.

I've always worked with strategic coaches and found their assistance invaluable, even if it drove me nuts. They taught me how to take those big leaps, even if they can seem like painful mistakes at times. When I started the magazine, it was a business venture. That was pretty straightforward. But I had always had the idea to grow it into the USCCA—and it was just a matter of time before that happened.

The question then becomes, "How?" *How* do you grow your business? (I think every business owner should be asking himself that question—all the time.) When I was working with Robert Hirsch out in Denver on how to transform the current business and we were spitballing ideas—some of which are still on the drawing table and we still plan to roll out—we started talking about how we needed to do something like the Self-Defense SHIELD. On a very basic level, it made a lot of sense: develop a program that protects our members if they're ever forced to defend themselves or their families with their firearms. The truth is, average responsible gun owners hope they'll never have to pick up their guns to defend themselves. But if they do, I really thought it made sense to provide them with something that would protect them from the inevitable legal issues that would follow.

I knew the NRA sold individual policies that were underwritten just like normal insurance policies, and so we wrote down the idea of providing that same benefit to our members. There were things I didn't like about the NRA policies and things I thought we could do better. I knew we could write an improved version that would better serve responsibly armed Americans.

Beyond that, it made strategic sense for the association—in serving the members as well as for the association to grow. It was a great member benefit that we didn't yet offer. Every business uses many of the same techniques. We were doing an exercise in concentric circles and looking at what USCCA members would possibly buy or use. These types of exercises are not big secrets—it's basic business development stuff.

So if we were to even consider offering an insurance benefit, the first step would be to find an insurance company stateside that would do it. Secondly, we wouldn't do it on an individual policy basis: we'd do it as a group policy.

I'm not ashamed to admit that I took a good look at what the NRA was offering. Why reinvent that wheel? But from there, we did it differently. We improved some things, discarded some things. We crafted a policy that we thought made more sense for people who carry.

And by this time, I was getting pretty good at "the drill." I went out and bought three books on liability and captive insurance. I needed to know what I was talking about if I was going to get an insurance company to listen to me. I figured it out.

But talk about a pattern that just kept repeating itself. Nobody would hear me out. I called on insurance company after insurance company and explained what I wanted. It was virtually an entirely new product, one they'd never heard about (let alone ever considered offering to anyone). It was mostly dead ends for me.

See, the insurance business is risk averse. They make money when they avoid risk. Instead, their business model is based on actuarial data…years of it. That's how they underwrite policies. So with a new policy, particularly one that they'd never offered before, they had zero actuarial data. It was a chicken-and-egg situation. They needed three, four, five years of actuarial data to even wrap their heads around writing this kind of policy, and they had nothing.

So I did the next best thing: I made it up. (Not made it up in the sense that I just pulled it out of thin air, but we did have a captive audience: our members.) We had thousands of people who could give us the data we needed. We actually polled our members and asked them a bunch of questions: Have you ever shot someone with a gun? How many times did you shoot them? Did you get sued?

It was a little ridiculous, but that's the kind of data they needed. It was just crazy in hindsight, but we really collected good quality data from our members.

Then, on a lark, I called my rep at our local insurance company. Now this was the place that I used for the silly little $500 policy I had in case our printer was ever stolen. He knew a guy who knew a guy who knew a guy who was at a company that wrote surplus line insurance. Essentially, his company underwrote things that nobody else wanted to.

They were willing to work with us. All we had to do was guarantee a certain number of participants. We rolled out the Self-

Defense SHIELD on June 6, 2011—the anniversary of D-Day. It wasn't a coincidence.

We originally gave members the option of whether or not they wanted to add the Self-Defense SHIELD benefit to their current Silver, Gold, or Platinum membership (which, at that time, was a subscription to *Concealed Carry Magazine* and exclusive access to a forum and a few other online resources). But so few people at that time had ever heard of self-defense insurance, so garnering interest in the new SHIELD product was slow-going. I really think it's just one of those things that people think they don't really need—or don't think about at all until it's too late.

And so I started to throw around the idea of eliminating the choice altogether. In fact, we had been advised, from a legal perspective, that we couldn't do a tiered membership where people could *choose* the option of adding the Self-Defense SHIELD. We had also been told that people couldn't just subscribe to the magazine (which was a member benefit) without being members. We know now that this wasn't exactly true, and we did have other options, but that's not what we had been told at the time. You can only make your decisions based on the best information you have available to you, and that's what we did.

And I'll be the first to admit that, in hindsight, maybe it wasn't the best way. But maybe it was. It certainly went down in USCCA history.

See, about a year later, all hell broke loose. We told all of our members that either they had to upgrade their memberships (to include the Self-Defense SHIELD) or simply ride out the remainder of their current memberships (and subsequent sub-scriptions to *Concealed Carry Magazine*).

We also broke the news that the cost of these new, plus-level memberships were *triple* what our members had been paying before they included the insurance-backed Self-Defense SHIELD. You can pretty much guess how well *that* went over initially. In all honesty, I don't think any of us were prepared for the backlash that followed.

We ended up losing half of our members. *Half,* as in 25,000 people. As their memberships expired, they just disappeared. Some were super irate and were posting in our forums. (For those of you who were around at that time, that was, indeed, me posting in response. I'd jump in once in awhile.) It was tough to see that and tough to see our membership drop.

But there was some irony to the whole situation. If you looked at the math, our revenue actually went up. We may have lost half our members, but the rest were paying triple the annual dues they'd been paying before the Self-Defense SHIELD had launched. It was a very unusual situation.

It was also hard because we really believed in what we were doing; we knew the Self-Defense SHIELD was a great idea and that, if our members ever needed it, they would be glad to have it in place. Of course, our members *today* recognize this fact, but that was probably the most frustrating thing for me back then: trying to relay just how important this benefit really was.

Beyond what's been legislated in the different states, the fundamental fact remains that none of us wants to use force to protect ourselves and our family, but we will do it if we have to. In those moments, we're not thinking about what happens when we're finally able to put the gun down. We're not thinking about the cops arriving or having to defend ourselves in court or what happens to our job if we end up being taken to jail while things get sorted out. All we're thinking about is ensuring that our family is safe. That's the way it should be, by the way. Our thinking needs to be crystal clear in those situations.

And that's where the Self-Defense SHIELD is so critically important. While the policy today is still fundamentally the same as when we rolled it out in 2011, the benefit is now up to $1.1 million per occurrence on the civil and criminal side. That seems like a lot of money, but trust me, the cost of defending yourself in court adds up very quickly. I don't know about you, but I don't have that kind of money just sitting around.

And honestly, that's what I love best about the Self-Defense SHIELD: it eliminates that risk—of jail, of bankruptcy—for hardworking, responsibly armed men and women who deserve to be celebrated—rather than punished—for their righteous acts of self-defense.

The way I see it, no one should have to "pass" on the responsibility of owning and carrying a gun just because he or she fears the legal and financial repercussions of that choice.

Think about this for a second: let's say you're not a member and you've defended yourself and your family against an intruder. He's now down in your front yard, incapacitated but still breathing. The neighbors heard a gunshot and have called the police. But wait, let's say nobody saw it happen besides you and the guy who is now lying in your front yard. Now what?

You're on your front porch, gun in hand, confused as all heck about what to do, adrenaline still pumping, shock setting in. But your family is safe inside the house, thank God. If you're calm enough, you've probably realized you not only need a lawyer, but a good lawyer. Do you have one? Do you call the guy who handled your mother's probate? The attorney whose kid plays on your son's baseball team? Are you supposed to go to the police station? What are you supposed to say? What is your wife supposed to do? If nobody has called for help for the man lying in your front yard, do you?

If you're not a USCCA member, this is a tough moment, probably one of the toughest you'll ever encounter. You absolutely did the right thing in stepping up and defending your family, but your life going forward, and that of your family, will never be the same.

If you *are* a USCCA member, you only have to do one thing: place a call to the USCCA Critical Response Team and our crisis managers take it from there. We have a team of people on staff that work around the clock, 365 days a year.

We get our members the best legal representation money can buy: attorneys who understand these types of legal cases. We also send up to $100,000 in instant cash for an attorney retainer, which we just increased from $10,000. Why? Why not? We can afford to extend that benefit to our members, and it's important to get the ball rolling right away. We don't want them to have *any* upfront out-of-pocket costs in the already terrifying aftermath of a self-defense shooting.

For me personally, it's important that the USCCA provides the best possible benefits to our members. I believe that protecting myself and my family is a natural-born right—*not* a financial decision. I never want to see a USCCA member on his porch debating whether or not to arm himself because he doesn't have enough money for his legal defense afterward. I want *all*

USCCA members to have that security ahead of time so they know they can exercise their rights—*without fear.*

That's what I love about what we do—when we can, we make things even better for our members.

IT WORKS

While we don't release data on member usage of the Self-Defense SHIELD, we can tell you it IS used, and relatively regularly.

Understandably, our members don't really like to talk about their experiences. By the time all is said and done, members have dealt with the police, the legal system, and usually even the media.

But we do sometimes hear stories. Recently, we had a USCCA member who heard his neighbor arguing with another man. That man went and got a bat and started beating the neighbor. Being a Good Samaritan, the USCCA member intervened, pulled out his gun, and told the bad guy to back off.

When the police arrived, they arrested the USCCA member instead of the man with the bat. It gets even worse: this happened on a weekend, and the USCCA member was supposed to start a new job that Monday. Can you imagine that call? "Sorry, I can't make it into my first day of work because I'm sitting in jail."

The USCCA member whipped out his card, called us, and did exactly what he was supposed to do. Our crisis manager matched him with good legal representation in his area and got him the money he needed right away to start taking care of the necessities, like posting bail. He was out of custody in less than 24 hours and was able to start his new job on time.

We knew we were on to something good, and our first claim helped prove it. The claim came in within the first three months of the launch and everything worked perfectly. The Self-Defense SHIELD helped reinforce what we already knew: the most dangerous place to live is in a world of denial.

If we actually took all of the members who have used the Self-Defense SHIELD since we rolled it out in 2011 and plotted them on a map, it would only show that it doesn't matter where you are geographically or what kind of neighborhood you live in: bad stuff happens *everywhere*. You can live in a perfectly middle-of-the-road neighborhood and wake up one night and have to protect yourself. Or you can live in the city. Or the country. Your address really doesn't matter at all. What matters most is that you understand that it *can* happen to you—and that you make the time to prepare for it if it does.

I have to be honest: it took almost two years for us to see our membership return to the level that it was at when we rolled out the Self-Defense SHIELD. I get that. Those early members had to see our vision and believe in what we were doing before they would come back.

What I appreciate most of all, though, are the members who stuck with us. When I went to the SHOT Show this year, I ran into a guy who had been a USCCA member since 2005. He told me he kept everything we'd put out over the years, which also probably means he has that keychain I sent out to get people to originally subscribe to the magazine. Without guys like that, we'd never be where we are today. I've met a bunch of them over the years, and it never ceases to amaze me just how much they support what we're doing and how much they know about the association and even about me.

One member I ran into was shocked to actually see me. He didn't even think I was a real person! Now *that's* funny. Who exactly did he think was behind all of this?

CHAPTER 7

FROM RELUCTANT LEADER TO ENTERPRISE BUILDER

*I joined the USCCA because if I ever need to defend myself
or my family I feel that I have a 'family' backing me up in terms of
all the legalities of a shooting. I grew up in Michigan and have been
a sportsman all my life. I have done some work in law enforcement
and the crime statistics today warrant being prepared to
protect oneself and one's family.*

– Dr. William W., OH

So there I was. The USCCA was getting back on track after the launch of the Self-Defense SHIELD, but I realized that internally, a lot of things still needed to change. I'd been forced to make some tough decisions in a very short period of time, relative to how long the USCCA had been in existence, and they were hard decisions. I'd made some mistakes too, but I could learn from those.

It was time to buckle down and make some internal changes. Our members, even now, don't really know what goes on behind the curtain. We're like any business. We have a physical office, people who come to work every day. But it wasn't always like that.

When I first started out, I was working from my kitchen table. That's pretty typical of any start-up business—it starts in your kitchen or in your garage or your basement. That's out of necessity. But as the USCCA grew in the beginning, I didn't always do things traditionally.

For example, I knew sales and marketing were important. They're important to any business. Anyone who says they aren't is lying. If you don't focus on sales and marketing, you're not in control of your own destiny. And yet, I've heard it all: "We don't do marketing. We just rely on word of mouth." I think that's absolutely crazy. Yep. That's just backwards.

Early on, I had a member named Pat who took an interest in what I was doing and he contacted me and asked if there was any way he could help. He knew concealed carry and he was good at what he did, so I hired him on as one of the first members of my sales and marketing team. Over time, I added a few more people, all similar types of guys, and they became my "virtual" marketing team. They were scattered across the country. At the time, our office was in Jackson, Wisconsin, and they had never set foot in it.

It turned out to be a very challenging situation.

Having a virtual marketing team worked fine in the early days, but as the business and number of employees grew, it got tougher and tougher. Please don't misunderstand; they were good guys. They absolutely had marketing skill and talent. They were so good that they helped me build the USCCA into what it is today. But everyone on the team working from all these different places instead of being together, hashing it out over a table? It just wasn't working for me.

Now, some people are very good at leading a virtual team. It happens all the time. But it wasn't happening for the USCCA or for me. I didn't have that skill set. It became a terrible Catch-22 for me. I had a team of people who did do and could do good work, but it wasn't turning into a scalable business solution for me.

That virtual sales and marketing team simply had to go. I realized that the USCCA really needed a more traditional structure for its marketing.

Don't get me wrong...there were definite tradeoffs. I had been able to assemble a great team of like-minded people who really understood what we were doing, but the progress just wasn't happening.

If you ask anyone here at the USCCA, I'm not about the 80-hour work week. In the beginning, sure, I put in 80+ hours because I had to get things going. But I don't think I've ever pushed that agenda on anyone else. That's never been part of the philosophy of our organization. You won't see that in our core values now (or ever, for that matter). I think it's important to have hobbies outside of work, to spend time with family, and really, to just enjoy life. But there also needs to be time dedicated to working hard and getting stuff done. It's all about balance. There's definitely room for both.

I slowly started to disband the virtual marketing team and started hiring on people in our office to take over that work. I told the offsite guys that either they move to Wisconsin to work in our office or their days as part of the team were numbered. A few guys decided to try it, but it didn't work out. I think it maybe had to do with what they were accustomed to—it's hard to make that change into a normal office with normal hours, particularly if that's not how you *like* to work.

There was one guy who I really hoped would change his mind, and even he wasn't interested. It wasn't an easy decision. It was tough as heck. Some of these guys had been with me for five years. They were experts in the art of persuasion for a mutual benefit, which is what marketing is. They knew what to say to me. But I wanted to establish an in-house marketing team; I wanted to grow the USCCA. I wanted to be able to sit down with the marketing team in one room and have these great sessions that would drive us forward. But at that point, it was just me at the table.

I remember when I finally did hire my first in-house marketing person. The few remaining offsite team members were always on him about something. They tortured him endlessly. But you know what? The in-house guy is still with me today. And those other guys? Long gone. It only solidified the fact that I was on the right track by forcing the offsite guys out and bringing new people in. Eventually, we were able to keep moving forward with a completely clean slate of people. And there was an even bigger upside for me personally: having people devoted to internal marketing efforts meant that I could step back on the day-to-day logistics and focus on the bigger picture.

Sometimes, at least from a marketing standpoint, our growth has happened in serendipitous ways. Yes, there's the direct marketing to members and potential members, but there's also marketing that increases people's awareness of you and your efforts.

Did you know the USCCA has its own radio show? The irony of this is that it's now carried in pretty much every radio market *except* Milwaukee, so we don't get it in our area.

It all started with Mark Walters, one of our very first members and one of the first guys who ever called me up and wanted to write for *Concealed Carry Magazine.* (He ended up writing a column called "The Ordinary Guy.") It didn't take long for me to realize that Mark was a talker. A big talker.

About two years into his stint as a columnist for the magazine, he had the opportunity to guest host on a weekly radio show. Now that was a perfect fit for someone like Mark, and it went really well. He did it again a month later and it soon became clear that there was some potential out there for our own radio show, which we ended up doing on a pay-to-play deal. We bought the time and locked it down on WGKA out of Atlanta, Georgia. Mark was all in about this idea: he went out and got himself an *Armed American Radio* tattoo on his arm that weekend and sold his trucking business shortly thereafter. I admired his commitment, that's for sure.

We ended up syndicating the show and went from zero to 25 to 36 radio stations pretty quickly after that. Even better—this deal also moved us out of the pay-for-broadcasting approach to actually selling advertising and bringing in a positive cash flow. I'm not knocking pay-to-play. That was a great first step for us, but we've really grown since then. Now, *Armed American Radio* is featured on more than 300 stations nationwide, and we just added a *Daily Defense* segment, which—you guessed it—airs daily. That was a huge step for us. It also speaks to the appeal of our show and the fact that we have an incredible audience all across the country.

Like I used to do with our website's online forum almost a decade ago, I do jump on the radio from time to time. It's kind of fun to call in once in awhile. It's one of those things I never imagined at the beginning of all of this, and it's kind of cool how it has progressed so naturally. Who would have thought that Timid Tim, the kid who lurked around the newspaper depot and was terrified to open his mouth, would call in to a national radio show and be comfortable talking in front of thousands of listeners? That's a really cool thing for me.

About a year ago, we decided to invest some money in public relations, and we hired a PR agency to increase our exposure. Public relations is hard. It really is about relationships and who you know and who THEY know and it takes a special kind of person to do it successfully. It's expensive, too.

This PR agency was trying to get us some exposure in radio and they asked me if I'd be willing to do that. It could be national markets or just some segment on a local radio show—I was pretty open to whatever they were able to get us as long as it was reasonably priced and worth my time.

So the PR lady called me up and she was VERY excited. Super excited. She had found the PERFECT radio thing for me: this *Armed American Radio* gig.

Yep, she had tried to book me on the USCCA's own radio show. You'd think she'd have done her homework on that one. But we did get a good laugh about it.

YES, THAT WAS ME ON THE PHONES AND IN THE FORUM

Even though I'm now the big-picture guy, I still pop up from time to time. Back in 2006 when we had our first website up and running, I really did jump in on the member forums. If you were a member back then, when things would get hot-and-heavy, sometimes I'd jump in on a thread. I loved watching the debates about our Second Amendment Rights. That was cool.

Though I don't do it as much now, I'll still occasionally answer the phone when people call in to our team. It is kind of fun surprising people and being able to say, "Yes, I really am Tim Schmidt and you really are talking to me."

Our internal team is great. I did all the hiring at first, and seriously, it was like the first few days with Tonnie. I said whatever I could to try to win the candidates over. I'm not going to lie. Some of it was complete bull. It wasn't that I was trying to be sneaky or be someone I wasn't. I really just wanted to make a good impression, and I was ready to promise the moon if it meant I could get good people in the door. At the end of the day, I genuinely wanted to put together a great team—and I was interviewing people that I knew could take us to the next level. I wanted people to believe in what we were doing— because I certainly did.

Over time, thankfully, our hiring process has really evolved. We do a fantastic job of bringing people on board now, and I'm not in charge of it. I definitely participate, but I'm not the gatekeeper anymore. That's a good thing for everyone. It's not easy to get through our hiring process—to actually get a job offer from us. We have an economy where people will say or do anything to get a job, and I get that. That's why we make the process so vigorous.

So, how *do* you work here? You'll probably go through four, five…even seven interviews. Our hiring decisions are based on objective analyses and on psychological and conative skills, which are things you ultimately can't fake or change. Still, at the end of the day, the sharpest people can get through all those walls, but if you're faking it, you will hate it here and you won't last.

Either you'll quit or you'll get fired. That's not fun for anyone—the candidates, our employees, or me, for that matter.

You know how I actually describe the USCCA to people who want to know what it's like to work here? We're basically Google with guns. That about sums it up.

We hire and fire on our core values, and they're important for our members to know. Why? Because our values affect how we serve our community.

I think they're worth sharing here, too:

CORE VALUE #1:
*We believe in what we do and we
communicate what we believe.*

First of all, you don't have to be a conservative or a Republican to work at the USCCA. I'm not. I'm a Libertarian. But you *do* have to believe that every American has the natural-born right to defend himself with whatever weapon he chooses.

Now, the next part is stickier. Any time you get a group of people together and there's interaction between those people, there's bound to be hurt feelings...especially if there's poor communication. You know what poor communication is? Miscommunication. Here, when the "hard stuff" needs to be said, it gets said.

We use a communication model that works. Basically, it's "I feel like [this] because of [this]: I want [this]." It actually works really well for communicating with anyone: your coworkers, your kids, your spouse. It arms you with a tool to communicate in a non-threatening way. It also stops you from stewing over things, because stewing sucks. It really does. The more you stew, the harder it is to communicate what you need to say.

Here's just a totally made up example. Let's say that we have a project that our graphic designer, Kelly, has been working on and it hasn't turned out. It's not up to our standards, it's late, and well, it's just not all that good. I could go to Kelly and completely chew her out, take the whole "What's wrong with you...?" approach.

But what does that do to Kelly? It immediately puts her on the defensive. It changes the whole tone of the situation. So what we try to do is something like this instead: "Kelly, I feel disappointed in how this project turned out because I know you are capable of doing a much better job and should have been able to meet this deadline. I want to be able to trust you."

This gives Kelly the opportunity to really think about what I'm saying and to respond in a similar fashion. She might say something like this:

"Tim, I'm feeling really frustrated over this project because you didn't get back to me with approvals on some of the elements, which means I couldn't actually complete the project on time. I want to have clear expectations."

I most likely would feel like a complete jerk and realize that yes, I did forget to do that. But the point is, we were able to communicate to each other why this project fell apart at the seams without putting each other on the defensive. Then, we can move on from it. Nobody stews and everyone feels better knowing that everything is out on the table.

CORE VALUE #2:
We are Highly Intelligent, Honest, Humble,
Happy, Hungry, and Healthy.

This is actually derivative of the book *Delivering Happiness* by Tony Hsieh. He's the founder of LinkExchange, which he sold to Microsoft for $265 million, and the current CEO of Zappos. You want a great shoe-buying experience? Go to Zappos!

When Hsieh was part of LinkExchange, he just hated it. He worked with a bunch of jerks. So when he built Zappos, he was absolutely obsessed with it being a place that he and others would *want* to come to everyday. Obviously, we all have days where we're just not feeling it. I certainly have days like that. But most of the time, I love coming to work. And I like to think the other people who work at the USCCA feel the same way. That's the kind of culture we have.

The list of things in this core value, which were inspired by Hsieh's work, really sum us up as a group of people and as an organization. I think when you can distill it down to these key things—seriously, who wouldn't want to be all of these?—success finds you, both in your personal and professional lives. Imagine the opposite: we are highly dim, liars who think a lot of ourselves, and by the way, we're unhappy, unmotivated, and unhealthy. Taking applications now!

CORE VALUE #3
We execute rapidly, systematically,
decisively, and fearlessly.

You know what destroys good ideas? Lack of momentum. This core value speaks to the most important aspect of having a successful business: speed of execution. Slow execution is like a cancer. Slow any idea down and it will turn into a crappy idea... or one that never gets off the ground at all.

When you look back at how things get done, it's obvious that almost everything can be executed faster. It's a law of the universe that almost any given task will expand to fill the time allotted to it. Why wouldn't it? We're trying to change that.

Only about 20 percent of any new ideas or projects will succeed. If you factor in the speed of getting stuff done, why wouldn't you want to burn through the 80 percent of ideas that will go nowhere and get to the stuff that will go somewhere? It's not the ideas that matter as much as the speed of getting to them. We never want to look back and see that we lost that chance to get to the two ideas that could have been great. We want to get stuff out the door, learn from what we did, and get on to the next iteration.

CORE VALUE #4
We believe that people and businesses are either growing or regressing. Our growth results from being aware and embracing change.

You know what's funny? I hate change. But this is a warning sign to me: when things stop changing, you're in trouble. In business—or in your personal life—it's always true.

Right now, we're working on changing something internally that directly affects about 10 people. Once we figure it out, it's going to rock their world. It's going to change how they do their work, but more importantly to them, it's going to significantly increase their value to the organization. Do we need to change it? No, we don't. But should we change it? Absolutely, because we can make it better.

And it's not change for change's sake—or whatever that cliché is. I think that's just some stupid comment made up by some guy in some department in some big company who doesn't want to change the way he's doing things because that's how things have always been done. I don't do anything *just* to change things, but I do believe that change is better than no change at all.

Here's how the thoughts go through my head: let's say I'm lying awake one night, thinking about how our financial reporting is not as efficient as it could be. I need to find a way to make it better. Why? It ties back to a basic entrepreneurial fear that the next biggest competitor out there is working in his garage right now, doing whatever I do, but doing it better. Every day, we need to make it harder and harder for that guy to compete with us.

Some of that is doing what's right and doing what's best. That's the "meat and potatoes" of staying successful, the business strategy. That's what separates a brilliant business from a business that just manages to stay afloat. We're lucky because we get to be creative to set the USCCA apart. We've broken so much new ground with what we actually do that it gives us the latitude to do some really cool stuff.

Like the time I gave away my truck. Or a gun a day for a month. It's all about finding new and exciting ways to do things.

Part of that idea is that I always like to one-up myself. If you're a USCCA member, you know what I'm talking about. You probably also know we're big on direct mail. Huge. We know it works for us. One of the ways to make a direct mail campaign successful is to appeal to the human psyche, and I can't think of anything more appealing than the idea of being able to win something really big. I think that holds true for marketing in general.

Think about when you were a kid and you went to a fair. After riding enough rides to turn your stomach into a blender, where was the next best place to go? The games, where just the potential of winning a stuffed animal bigger than yourself was enough to make you blow all the spending money you brought along.

There are legalities to these kind of campaigns, though. You have to open up giveaways to anyone who wants to enter, regardless of if he or she buys something or not. That's why you always see "no purchase necessary" on sweepstakes and whatnot.

So we were sitting there trying to outdo ourselves on our latest giveaway and I looked out the window and said, "Hey, what about my truck?" There was nothing wrong with it, except that it was getting to be about two years old and I wanted to replace it. It had a market value of about $40,000, and I was about to trade it in for the same truck but a new model. I'm pretty stuck in my ways, I guess.

Well, yeah! That seemed like a pretty good idea. Win Tim's truck! That's not something you see very often. The USCCA team members thought it was great too, so we went with it. The response? Fantastic.

Now, even though we had to open the contest to everyone, I can tell you honestly that I was very glad when a *Concealed Carry Magazine* subscriber won my truck. I couldn't have picked a better home for it. The guy was from Owatonna, Minnesota. He used to install sprinkler systems, but he'd just been laid off. I got to make the call telling him he won, and—of course—he didn't really believe it at first. Who would? But we made the call and this guy and his wife drove from Owatonna to West Bend, Wisconsin—their first vacation in the 10 years they'd been married—and we covered the taxes with some extra money so they wouldn't have to worry about that either.

It's kind of funny—people still talk about it. I was at a meeting for the local Boys & Girls Club and I drove up in my new truck (which looks exactly like my old truck) and someone said, "Hey, I'm a USCCA member. I thought you gave that truck away?"

We then had the idea to give away a gun a day for a month. We got all sorts of publicity from that. Some bad publicity, of course, including *USA Today*. But would we do that again? Heck yes! (The truth is, we're coming up on our *fourth* Gun-a-Day promotion. It's pretty much a tradition at this point.)

It doesn't have to be some grand idea, either. It can be something really simple and brilliant. We recently did a promotion and we really wanted to hit it out of the ballpark, so we said that the first 2,500 people who bought would get a signed copy of our book, *Concealed Carry and Home Defense Fundamentals*. Great idea, right? Wrong. Guess who had to sit down and put his signature on 2,500 books? That stops becoming fun almost immediately. But it's situations like that that are really very humbling and flattering to me. I feel like it's my duty to not take them for granted.

But even though that was really awesome and I did succeed at one-upping myself, we're kind of moving away from giveaways now. We realized if we didn't stop, we were running the risk of turning things into a circus. And that takes the focus away from what the USCCA is *really* about. So now we're focusing our efforts on investing in things that really matter to *all* of our members. When we make things more efficient, our employees benefit and our members benefit. I can't think of two better reasons than those, right there.

I have to admit, though, it still was fun to see my truck drive away.

CORE VALUE #5
We believe in accountability, and in holding each other responsible to achieve our goals.

This core value? It's sort of a permission slip to call people out. It's a natural human trait to want to avoid embarrassment. But we need to hold people accountable. It's a step in the direction of performance transparency.

We have a weekly meeting here. We actually call it the "Oh Shit!" Meeting. Seriously, that's the official name of it. It's designed to make sure everyone feels comfortable saying what needs to be said. Now when you have 40 people who sit there and don't raise their hands, you know that's not working. But I think we do a pretty good job of making people feel comfortable to say what's on their minds. We also have an anonymous component that employees can use. Do I think people speak as freely as they would like to? That I don't know. I'm sure there are times when they decide not to say something, particularly if it is about me or about something they don't think I'm doing right. But the point is that we try pretty darn hard to make everyone feel the same level of accountability.

WHY ARE WE SUCCESSFUL?

It's because of the 70-plus people we have working behind the scenes that the USCCA is the success that it is. And it's the changes that we've made on the inside that make the changes we've experienced outside of the walls even better. I may be the person who everyone recognizes and who got the ball rolling, but there's a whole team of people that works together to make these things happen.

We have a lot going on, and I'm not going to give away any secrets, because that proverbial guy working in his garage on the next "bigger and better" idea is probably reading this book. But we're always looking at ways to change things and make them better. One thing we just started this year is our Concealed Carry Expo. We held the first one right down the road from us at our county fairgrounds.

See, we're really careful about what we offer our members. We're an association, and we could be continually tacking on outside benefits. (Associations like to do things like that. But every little car rental discount dilutes the value of a membership.) Our biggest and most important benefit is, and will always be, the Self-Defense SHIELD. But we think adding the Expo was a fantastic idea. It creates an in-person experience for our members as well as the general public. I remember when I was starting out on my own concealed carry journey and the bad experiences I had. We want to ensure it isn't that way for anyone who wants to take on the responsibility of protecting their loved ones with a gun. Basically, any benefit we decide to offer our members goes right back to our focus: helping them keep their families safe. That's why people join the USCCA in the first place.

It's great that the USCCA has also reached a point where we can see huge changes.

Take the first SHOT Show I attended and the last SHOT Show I attended…it's a night and day difference.

That first SHOT Show, when everyone looked at me like I was crazy and I went home with almost as many magazines as I had come with, it was just me and my dad.

At the 2015 show, we actually had a booth and 17 employees with us. The fact that we actually had exhibit space at all was a very big deal. (There are more than 1,000 people on the waiting list to exhibit.) Though I had finagled my way in that first year, 2015 was our first year as an exhibitor. Let me tell you, it was a lot cooler this time around.

We're a little different because we're not really selling something tangible at these shows. We're not selling guns or ammunition like a lot of the big names in the industry. People don't come to our booth to see the latest and greatest. It's quite humbling to me because people actually come to the booth to see me—to see the people behind the USCCA. They really don't believe I'm a real person. There's something fun in that, to see people recognize me from our website or our videos and put two and two together. It's like something just clicks: "Hey! Tim *is* real and he's standing right there." It's cool to see people's expressions and reactions, and it honestly cracks me up a little. What these people probably *don't* know is that I'm just as excited to see *them*. I know how many members we have, but it's still a great feeling to be able to talk with an individual member to see how much we have in common and how we share the same beliefs. I don't think that will ever go away for me.

My perspective in the booth is pretty unique. When our members walk in, I can tell it immediately by the look in their eyes. They feel they know me.

IT EVEN HAPPENS AT HOME

When my daughter Dagny was in kindergarten, Tonnie started teaching Sunday School. I wasn't really available to be there, so she did it with another member of our parish. Early on, they were just making polite conversation and the woman asked Tonnie about our family and what I did.

We didn't know it at the time, but the woman checked out our website and she signed up. She got all of our stuff—the good, the bad, the videos, the personal stories about me and my family. You name it, she got it.

Eventually I was able to get a little more involved. One Sunday, I showed up, and I saw that same look in this woman's eyes when she met me. She had a big smile on her face and she greeted me like a long lost friend. She said, "Hi, Tim! I just feel like I've known you forever!"

If people know of the USCCA, they know me. And it is true; it is my story. I have no problem with that at all. There's so much upside to that if I can connect to the person. I think it would be difficult to head an organization like the USCCA without being open about your own family and your values. All of our members have a lot in common with each other—and with me. Concealed carry and the right to arm yourself is a personal issue, and I know I would have a difficult time buying into an organization where I didn't know anything about the head of it or how he protects his own family. When you read about my family, everything you read is true. I do have three kids and two dogs and a lawn to mow and the things you read about do happen in our lives.

I think a lot of our members would have liked to have taken the path I did with the USCCA, but they didn't know how to start on their own, and that's *exactly* why we're here. They like the fact that they can ride along with me and can connect with what I'm doing. That's an awesome feeling to have that trust and support. But the weird thing is that I'm totally the same person that our members see in the magazine and on the videos and at the shows. If you ran into me on the street in West Bend or at my daughter's dance performance or in a restaurant, that's me. Same guy.

So when I'm in the booth, I want to make sure that I'm available and present to any member who takes the time to come up and talk with me. But here's the problem. There are two kinds of people at a trade show: the kind of people who thrive on the interaction, who draw energy from other people, and who think working a trade show is fun. And then there's the other kind: the people who have the energy sucked out of them when they meet people. I'm the second kind. It's like the people come into the booth and take a little bit of me with them. By the end of the day, I'm just exhausted. But whether someone comes into the booth at 9 a.m. or at 4 p.m., it's really important to me to greet them with a smile and a good handshake. They make a big deal out of meeting me, and I want to make a big deal out of meeting them. That's basically it right there.

I get a thrill out of meeting people, too. I met Ted Nugent for the first time in 2006, and he is a great example of a guy who treats every single person waiting in line to see him the way I want to treat people. He's also a what-you-see-is-what-you-get guy. He's pure Ted. I respect that. I've met Glenn Beck and Sean Hannity, too. I guarantee you that our mailing list is bigger than Sean Hannity's, but I would never walk into his office and not think it was a big deal to meet him. He's so good at what he does. Absolutely I want to meet people like that...and that's how I want people to feel about me.

How far have we come since that first SHOT show? In 2008, we hosted our first VIP dinner. We had five writers from four magazines show up. We didn't have reservations anywhere and we ended up taking them to Jimmy Buffett's Margaritaville, sitting in the middle of a room surrounded by people. Half the table was wondering what to say to each other and the other half was wondering who was going to pay for dinner.

This year, we had reservations at one of the nicest steak joints in Las Vegas. The VIP dinner actually included VIPs—potential business partners, some of our most prolific writers, people from the Second Amendment Foundation—and it has evolved into a very cool event. That's the way I view the USCCA as well. Beyond all the important work the USCCA does, it's a very cool association to belong to, and it just keeps getting better.

I like to think that *I* keep getting better, too. As the USCCA has evolved, so have I. I've shifted gears a little. I've definitely stopped looking for a "bigger and better" idea to pursue. And honestly? It's a terrific feeling to know that I've finally found what I want to do. I'm much more content, that's for sure, but I'm still constantly looking for ways to improve myself. And I think that's a good thing.

During the past few years, I've also spent a lot of time thinking about what I believe in. After some thought, I was able to come up with some pretty clear ideas, which hang on my office wall. Anyone who comes in to visit me can read them:

I BELIEVE

I believe that most people are inherently good.

I believe that when given a chance, most people will do the right thing.

I believe that most Americans will do anything for their families.

I believe in God.

I believe that opportunity is usually disguised as hard work.

I believe that the free enterprise system is a gift from God.

I believe that the ability to forgive and forget will set you free.

I believe that the harder you work, the luckier you get.

I believe in Liberty.

I believe in choosing to be happy.

I believe in accepting responsibility for everything that happens to me.

I believe that every challenge or obstacle is an opportunity to become a better person.

I believe that life can be tough, but at the end of the day, life is what you make of it.

I believe in my Family.

I believe that evil exists. It just does.

I believe that it is my responsibility to protect all that is good from all that is bad.

I believe in preparing for the worst while expecting the best.

I believe in the natural-born and inalienable right to self-protection.

I believe that the man or woman who shirks their duty to defend and protect simply doesn't understand their true responsibility as a God-fearing and freedom-loving American.

I believe in myself.

I believe that a gun cannot be good or bad. It is simply a thing. A tool.

I believe that the founders of our country used these tools that we call guns to liberate themselves from tyranny and start the greatest experiment in freedom that the world has ever seen.

I believe the statistics that tell us responsibly armed, law-abiding Americans use guns over 2,739 times EVERY DAY to defend their lives and the honor of their loved ones.

I believe in being peaceful and avoiding conflicts at all costs. But when conflict comes after me and pushes me into a corner, I believe in fighting as if the lives of my wife and children depend on it...because they do.

This is what I believe.

CHAPTER 8

THE 'ANTI-GUN' CRITICS

I joined the USCCA because the anti-gun folks clearly have a lot of shout power, from the President on down. People who carry concealed need unified shout power, too—as well as practical guidance on such matters as equipment, training, and legal defense. The USCCA is the only place where I could find that whole package in one organization.

– Richard V., SC

It doesn't matter what you do in life; you'll always have critics. When you're the face of a concealed carry association and you publicly state that you have the right to protect yourself and your family...well, let's just say that there are people out there who, for whatever reason, oppose those things. Not everyone believes in the natural, God-given right to keep and bear arms.

I can't say that I really understand that position—and I certainly don't agree with it—but who am I to tell someone else what they should believe? The Bill of Rights affirms a number of personal freedoms: chief among them are the right to keep and bear arms and the right to free speech, and we're all free to believe or not believe in these things. I, personally, prefer to believe in things that I know are true and that I can have faith and confidence in. But I also recognize that for every person out there fighting for our rights, there is another person equally as passionate about trying to strip them away.

And honestly, between the outright lies, misinformation, and bullying tactics used by anti-gunners, *very* few things surprise me anymore.

But here's the deal: their whole argument is fundamentally silly.

This may shock everyone when I say this, but I really believe that those of us who carry and those who fall under the anti-gunner umbrella...well, we all want the same thing. We want to be safe and we want our families to be safe. We have the same goals, but we're trying to reach those goals on two *very* different —opposing—paths.

Take, for example, gun-free zones. Responsibly armed Americans know that these don't work, because—you guessed it!—*criminals don't follow the law.* Bad guys respect these signs as much as they respect any other law or ordinance on the books. (In other words, they *don't.*) But somehow, people who oppose guns and self-defense continue to think of these places as "safety" zones. I shudder at that thought, because nothing could be further from the truth.

The bottom line is that gun-free zones serve only to disarm the law-abiding.

Take USCCA members, for example. They're very conscious of gun-free zones because they're law-abiding people. How do I know this? Because I know our members. See, we believe in our laws; they exist for the good of society. So while we may not like them, we still follow them. That's why you won't find most of us carrying in gun-free zones: because we have a healthy respect for laws and for the rights of business owners.

Now, I'm sure some of our members go out in public and see a gun-free zone sign posted in the window of a restaurant or at a shopping mall or wherever and make a trip back to the car, pop the trunk, unholster, and secure their guns.

But I think it's probably more accurate to say that the majority of our members see those signs and keep on driving to places that *do* allow guns.

The simple truth is that we are not safe in gun-free zones. And that's why I cannot, in good conscience, tell my kids—or anyone else, for that matter—to let down their guards in these places.

Gun-free zones are easy targets for criminals. I mean, what better place for bad guys to go than where they can be certain the good guys are unarmed?

You know, that's something the critics completely fail to understand: that it's not *good guys* with guns who are going around shooting other people. That line of thinking frustrates me to no end. And yet it seems that anytime there is an irresponsible or tragic situation involving a gun—particularly one that happens at a school—our critics assume that the shooter is one of us.

Let's get one thing straight: responsibly armed Americans are the good guys. And good guys with guns do not go around shooting people.

No, it's not the man with a concealed carry permit who's out there causing problems. It's not the single mom who took the concealed carry class and who keeps her gun in her purse for her own safety who's out there causing problems.

No. These people are the good guys. And honestly, I'm sick and tired of them bearing the blame for the wrongdoings of a bunch of really bad apples.

You wouldn't know it to listen to our critics, but our hearts hurt just as much as theirs do when something like Sandy Hook happens. Or a Marysville Pilchuck in Washington State. That incident was far more complex and difficult to unravel: instead of 26 victims, there were five. It seemed to have involved a failed teenage romance. All of the victims were close friends, and some were related. It didn't get as much play in the media, but it should have. Not only was that situation devastating to the community, it also had to have shattered that family.

But it's interesting to use it as an example of why people like us believe that the right to protect ourselves is so important.

Although attitudes toward this are changing a bit, teachers generally aren't allowed to carry; they give up that basic right the minute they walk onto school grounds. But who stopped the Marysville Pilchuck shooting from continuing? An unarmed, first-year teacher. She released a statement to the media that said, in part, "I reacted exactly like all my colleagues would in this type of event. I am a schoolteacher, and like all teachers, I am committed to the safety and well-being of my students."

I am committed to the safety and well-being of my family, and that commitment extends beyond my home. When my three kids go to school or go off to the mall or are in public places, I still feel the same way. No matter how old they get, I don't think that will ever go away. I'm their dad, and it's my duty to keep them safe.

138

And if you took a survey of USCCA members, I don't think you'd find a single statement that we more universally believe in. *Nothing* is more important than protecting our families.

Now, not everyone is cut out for that role. It's one that requires both courage and action in the face of danger. Just imagine the mindset that young, *unarmed* teacher in Washington had to have had to walk up to an *armed* teenager and stop him. How many people would have run in the other direction? Not only did this teacher walk into (instead of out of) the cafeteria, she went straight up to the shooter and she tried to stop him from harming others and himself. The teacher took action, and it made all the difference. Who knows how many lives she saved by that choice.

Now, let's take this a step further. Imagine if this responsible young woman, someone who clearly has proved she's worth her mettle, was able to carry on school grounds. She approached the shooter when he was in the act of reloading. His intentions were pretty clear at that point, and the last life he took was his own as she tried to stop him. If she'd had a gun, could she have saved him? Could she have saved more of those students?

We'll never know the answer to these questions, but we *do* know this: in the chaos of the Marysville Pilchuck lunchroom that day, this teacher was in a classroom nearby and beat the school safety officer (who was probably armed with a flashlight at most) to the scene. She arrived before the police officers, before the fire department...before *any other person* who was formally trained to protect her.

Full disclosure: I don't know this teacher. I don't know if she'd even want to carry. But man, do I have the utmost respect for her and what she did. But still, I can't help but think how differently things *could* have turned out if she had been properly armed and trained to protect herself and her students.

Now the anti-gunners would think that's a crazy idea. But it's not. What's crazy is that across America, we can safely protect our families in our own homes—and yet we send our kids to school where equally responsible adults lose that freedom. Every day, you and I send our kids off to school and hope that the unthinkable never happens. We hope that our teachers will be able to get them out of harm's way until help arrives.

But it doesn't always happen that way...and it's terrible.

Nope. Instead, we have to rely on the inadequate "crisis" training our school teachers and administrators receive, which quite honestly leaves them—and our children—defenseless in such situations.

Students and teachers are taught to "lock down," to wait for help to arrive. It's ironic in a way, because it fights our natural and instinctual fight-or-flight response. Essentially, our children aren't allowed to do either. They just have to sit quietly and wait. That's their "best-case" scenario. I'm sorry, but that's not good enough for me—or for my kids.

Now, I realize that not every teacher out there would be willing to carry a gun. Arming oneself takes a lot of courage—and it's a *huge* responsibility. A life-changing one, in fact. But if there are *some* teachers out there who would be willing to make that commitment, to accept the call to be responsible armed Americans, imagine how the equation would change. Their only option would no longer be barricading the doors and shutting off the lights and waiting. No...they'd be able to fight back.

I think our children deserve at least that much. It sounds harsh, and it is, but what they don't deserve is to sit around and wait to die.

The concept of gun-free zones only makes sense in a perfect, ideal world. But this is also a world where airline flights are always on time, there is never a traffic jam, nobody ever overcooks the turkey on Thanksgiving, and it never rains on any parades, baseball games, or on the day I'm planning to mow the lawn. Our world is too unpredictable—and too chaotic—to believe that putting up a sign will stop someone who wants to carry a gun with the express intent to harm people with it.

Think of it this way: in every classroom, probably a little more than half of the class follows the teacher's rules all of the time. These are the kids who understand that following the rules is the right thing to do. Then there's probably about another quarter of kids who try very hard to pay attention and get their homework in on time. They succeed most of the time, but can sometimes end up in the weeds. Then there's the remaining quarter of the class. These are the kids who just drive teachers crazy: they never get their homework done, they get no support from home, and school is just a good time (or a place to pass the time) for them. The teacher is lucky, despite his or her best efforts, if these kids get average grades.

And then in each classroom, there are one or two kids who just don't play by the rules at all. Nobody really wants to sit by them or partner with them. They never turn any homework in and they're destructive, disrespectful, and disruptive. Why? Because they don't have any respect for authority or for the rules. In these kids' minds, those rules don't apply to them.

That's exactly why our critics fail. They're fighting the wrong people. They're essentially punishing the whole class instead of dealing with the few individual bad apples.

Now, I understand that there will always be critics of freedom. They're afraid of it and they don't understand it. And most of all, they don't want the *responsibility* for it. But you know what? That's fine. There are others—people like you and me—who answer that call and have the courage to take it on.

By the very nature of what we do, the USCCA falls victim to these anti-freedom critics. To be honest, we've always had them, and I don't expect that to change anytime soon. But that doesn't mean that some things still don't disappoint me. Here's a recent example:

If you were lucky enough to attend Super Bowl XLIX, you probably bought a program and took it home as a souvenir. I bet one of the first things you noticed was our ad. Pretty powerful stuff, huh? Memorable and thought provoking, just the way we hoped it would be.

Oh, wait. You didn't see it? That's right, nobody did. The NFL refused to run it unless we made some major changes—like using "USCCA" instead of "United States Concealed Carry Association." (Apparently they didn't want *any* reference to guns or carrying a gun...because, you know, that might offend a few people.)

It was a great ad. It's still a great ad. It was a picture of a dad and his two kids, and the message was simple: Are you doing everything in your power to keep your loved ones safe? Our model dad was, because he was carrying. We were promoting an idea—how to protect yourself and your loved ones.

But the NFL wasn't "comfortable" with the holstered gun on the dad's hip. You can check it out for yourself above.

After going back and forth numerous times, we had enough and decided to pull the plug on what turned out to be less of an opportunity and more of a reminder that some people just don't get it.

What baffled me more than anything, though, was the obvious hypocrisy at play. This would be the same sports organization that constantly fends off PR nightmares with its players. It's pretty safe to say that the average USCCA member isn't involved in dog fighting or domestic abuse or child abuse...and we're proud to say that neither Plaxico Burress or Jovan Belcher have ever been card-carrying members of our organization. (If you're not a football fan, you probably don't know who these guys are. While out partying in a nightclub, New York Jets wide receiver Plaxico Burress shot himself in the leg. Jovan Belcher, a linebacker for the Kansas City Chiefs, shot his girlfriend and then, in a completely separate incident, committed suicide in front of his coach and general manager. Unfortunately for both of these guys, they're better known now for what they did off the field than what they did *on* it.)

Members of the USCCA are among the most conscientious in the world when it comes to firearms safety and personal responsibility. That irony was lost on the NFL advertising decision makers, and it made me mad.

But sometimes, the right thing to do is to walk away. You can't argue with stupid, and we weren't going to be bullied into whitewashing an idea that is so central to what the USCCA stands for—and pay for it to boot.

This NFL situation was part of a larger opportunity presented to us to advertise in several sports related programs put out by NASCAR, the NBA, the NHL, and the NFL. It *could* have been a great marketing vehicle for us if all of these organizations really understood us and what we were trying to do.

Luckily, one of them did. We ended up advertising in the NASCAR 2015 Annual Racing Preview. The ad looked great, and we received a ton of positive feedback. I guess I'm just dumbfounded by the fact that one sports organization could be completely on board with what we do and another one could just be so completely blind.

I guess it's safe to say that anti-gunners confuse the heck out of me. I just don't understand their criticism at all.

Here's another example: Moms Demand Action for Gun Sense in America.

Now, I really wish I could say something nice about this group. After all, I'm a parent, too—and I'm all about gun sense and gun safety. The problem is that *my* definition of gun sense and *their* definition of gun sense is a night and day difference.

See, Moms Demand Action likes to pull the proverbial "mom" card—"guilting" their opponents by using the "if you cared about the kids" argument. Well, I care about my kids; that's *exactly* why I *do* carry a gun. Groups like this want to take away my right to choose *how* I care for and protect my kids and my family. Sorry, Moms: no one gets to decide that but me. (By the way: Moms Demand Action isn't really a grassroots effort by a bunch of moms opposed to guns. It's a group funded by the deep pockets of some very high profile people with certain political leanings.)

This is also the group that targeted Kroger, the nation's largest grocery store chain, last year. (We don't have Krogers in Wisconsin, but I paid close attention to what went on because this could really happen anywhere: your local Publix or Meijer— or in my neck of the woods, Pick 'N Save.)

According to *Bearing Arms,* "[Moms Demand Action's] goal [was] to accomplish through bullying what they [couldn't] establish through legislation: reducing the number of places that law-abiding citizens [could] exercise their basic human right to self-defense."

The move was in large part a social media stunt, one that grossly skewed the organization's efforts to petition Kroger into banning open carry in their stores. I guess when logic isn't on your side, there isn't much left to do besides beg for what you want.

What I found especially amusing was the Twitter hashtag that Moms Demand Action used to prop up their social efforts: #GroceriesNotGuns.

If we had wanted to go tit-for-tat on this, I guess the USCCA could have started its own social campaign, petitioning the Krogers of the world to demand concealed carry in their stores. We could have made our social hashtag #GroceriesAndGuns. Now *that* would have been something. But in all seriousness, I'd much rather rely on the facts. And the facts prove that good guys with guns help stop bad guys with guns.

What infuriates me to no end is how our critics lump *all* people with guns into one group. It's completely illogical, and yet they don't see any difference between us and the bad guys. So they push for laws and initiatives and changes that punish *everyone.*

And the media? They perpetuate this blurred line.

There is a big difference between what responsibly armed Americans stand for and do and what hits the news. Law-abiding men and women with guns are not the bad guys; they're not out there challenging law enforcement or using guns to express their dislike of government or going on unexplainable rampages.

And yet, we never hear the good guys' stories. We never hear about the single mom who protects her children from a home invader. We never hear about the lives saved when a concealed carry permit holder stops an armed carjacker.

No. All we hear are the bad guys' stories...and these stories give our critics the fuel they need to keep pushing their anti-gun agendas.

And yet, hateful rhetoric and big-pocketed funders have done *nothing* to address the problems we have in this country.

What *does* help address these problem is what the USCCA—what people like you and me—are doing: educating and training people how to defend themselves and their families.

I've said it before, and I will keep saying it until the sun goes down: *good citizens do not break the law.* They do not resist arrest. And they do not seek revenge for circumstances they perpetuate through their violent acts.

No, if a law-abiding citizen chooses to own a gun, he or she buys it legally and obtains the proper licensing.

Good citizens do not break the law.

The bottom line is that our critics just don't get it. Maybe it's because they don't understand freedom. Maybe it's because they don't *want* to accept responsibility for their own safety. Or maybe it's because they aren't willing to recognize that there are other worthwhile, meaningful opinions than just their own. (There are people out there who seriously spend their entire lives believing that *they* are the only ones with the right opinion; they think it's their job to not only suppress any opposing opinion, but to deny the right to have one at all.)

There's more, too: an armed society means recognizing that evil exists—and some people want to ignore that. They want to believe that it can't or won't happen to them. But as Lt. Col. Dave Grossman is fond of saying, "Hope is not a strategy."

The funny thing is, I don't doubt that almost every single anti-gunner would jump in, without even a bit of hesitation, to protect their loved ones. It's just that they don't see firearms as a viable way to do that. But if they were *really* faced with a violent criminal, wouldn't they do anything and everything in their power to ensure the ones they love would make it out alive...even if that meant using a gun? Why wouldn't you want to give yourself and your family the best possible chances of survival?

I wish I could get our critics to understand this point.

My whole life—and I think you'll agree with me here—is based on the notion that guns are what allow me to protect my family. Responsibly carrying a gun is not an unreasonable or crazy idea. It is—and should be—an option for anyone who's willing to accept it. And no one should be able to take that away; it's a God-given right. I really don't care how much someone tries to bully me into believing otherwise: I simply refuse to bend on that point.

CHAPTER 9

FREEDOM

One of my favorite quotes is Thomas Jefferson's: 'The beauty of the Second Amendment is you won't need it until they try to take it from you.' I believe USCCA is educating us to protect our right to defend against tyranny.

– Michael S., VA

I think it's pretty easy to define freedom. I personally take a pretty Libertarian view of it: don't hurt others and don't steal their stuff. That's freedom to me in a nutshell. As long as you're not infringing on others' inalienable rights, you should be able to do whatever you want.

It doesn't get much simpler than that.

But our freedom as Americans does have a pretty interesting history, and it goes right back to the U.S. Constitution and our Bill of Rights. I personally think these documents were divinely inspired—you can see it in the words and the intent. If you go through the history of mankind, there has never been a country that exemplifies productivity as much as we do. Nor has there been a country that has accumulated so much wealth in such a short amount of time.

Our Founding Fathers were godly men. (Well, most of them were. James Madison was a communist, in my opinion.)

Look at Thomas Jefferson and Benjamin Franklin—who they were and how they operated. Franklin was quite an entrepreneurial fellow. He wrote an entire essay called "The Way to Wealth," and more than 230 years later, everything he says still makes sense. He was an advocate of working hard and working smart.

What our Founding Fathers did was create a document that provided the ground rules for our country. They also created a living document, and they left room for adjustment and change as our country grew. Think of the foresight they had to have had in doing that. How could they have possibly known what America could and would become?

It's important for us as modern Americans to understand our roots.

The concept of freedom has been a work in progress, and it has taken many years for this concept—as a universal right—to develop. It's not an American idea, but America certainly took the idea and ran with it.

The ancient Greek philosophers thought about freedom. Plato talks about it in *The Republic.* He professed concepts of self-governance, though they were pretty utopian in nature. The Roman Republic was based on the concept of representative government with a constitution and three branches of government—sound familiar? Even back then, this form of government recognized natural rights, including self-defense.

If you quickly look at history, while there were isolated instances of representative government, and governments that valued liberty, they weren't prevalent or enduring. The rights of the individual rarely were a priority—or just flat out didn't exist—particularly during the era of sovereign kings and nobility. Think about that for a minute.

If you weren't part of the nobility or their households and you weren't among the monarch's hand-picked nobility, your chances of gaining any sort of personal freedom were quite limited. Lower nobles only tended to receive rights due to bartering—you scratched the monarch's back, now he'll scratch back a little. Maybe you received some land or some rights, but it was never a natural-born right. It was bestowed on you. And God forbid you were a slave, serf, or commoner, because freedom would be in short supply for you. You had fewer rights than the monarch's livestock. Education, enlightenment, thought, economic opportunity, social mobility, even freedom of religion…those really wouldn't exist for you.

Fast forward a few centuries and, during the Renaissance, things started to change. This was the period of Enlightenment, and the concept of the individual man—with his own individual rights—started to appear. People started to ask questions, to create and express their ideas, without fear of repercussion. The Enlightenment took the idea of natural law and ran with it: it was the law that existed by nature and was universal to all. It used reason to analyze human nature and defined the rules of moral behavior, independent of who was in charge or control. It superseded civil law or sovereign law, and it made the fight against both morally and ethically correct. That's a revolutionary idea, and though the concept of America was still to follow more than a century later, it was part of the framework that led those first Europeans to North America.

It was about that time that the concept of freedom really started to take hold. One of the first original thinkers in philosophy of natural law was John Locke. He was English, but we can excuse him of that, because he constructed some important concepts of individual freedom and liberty, including self-defense. Feel free to look him up—even more than 350 years later, his writings make a lot of sense. His words and concepts are echoed in the works of our Founding Fathers and the fledgling United States of America.

Today, the average person doesn't think about this a whole lot. We take these freedoms for granted. But think about what life was like as an early colonist, circa the late 1700s. You're part of a group of people like no other—you're starting a brand-new nation based upon individual freedoms. That's a concept diametrically opposed by your king. So what does he do? He comes and takes away your guns and your ability to defend yourself.

What the colonists did was brilliant. They would fight, of course, but they also used words: *We hold these truths to be self-evident, that all men are created equal, that they are endowed by their Creator with certain unalienable Rights, that are among these Life, Liberty, and the pursuit of Happiness.*

Those words are from the Preamble to our Declaration of Independence, and they really mean what they say—don't let anyone tell you otherwise. And what's so beautiful is that they can be read directly and mean exactly the same today as they did nearly 240 years ago. Our Founding Fathers were extremely particular and extremely precise about what they wanted to say—that's why these words transcend time and geography. They were speaking about all Americans—dead, alive, and yet to be born. That's pretty powerful when you think about it.

Honestly, I think if you really look at who has come to America since that first generation, it doesn't really matter what country they emigrated from. They all had that desire for freedom, to go to a country where that was so clearly recognized. I think that's true of my own family, whom I don't particularly know much about. I wish I did—the only story I know is about my great grandmother, who came over in the 1920s and refused to set foot on a boat again, even though she lived on a lake. She had had enough on the passage over to America.

But what I can tell you about my family is probably similar to your family—they were in search of freedom. I don't think the average American appreciates that. When my family left Europe, they were taking a risk, and I think all those immigrants that arrived in America during those years of growth were natural risk takers. They could have stayed put wherever they were, but they knew there was no opportunity there for them. There was no freedom. And they wanted freedom.

Think about this: look at the number of businesses that were started by those first generation Americans, regardless of where they settled. They brought their trades from their countries— the woodworkers and the seamstresses and the bricklayers and the butchers—and they came here, usually with next to nothing, and they worked their butts off. Why? Because they had the freedom to do it. Nobody could really stop them— there was no monarch or political party to restrict them; their religious affiliation didn't strip them of that freedom either.

As a nation, I think we have a national desire for freedom, even though we may not always be consciously aware of it. As free humans, we have a natural right to many things, and among them is the natural-born right to protect our families and ourselves.

If you actually look at the Second Amendment, it was written to protect us against tyranny. Taking this historical perspective, it really makes a lot of sense, and it explains why our Founding Fathers were so clear about it. What else could it mean? Back then, when England didn't believe how deep our convictions were to this freedom, we were able to show them with our arms and some pretty good guerilla tactics. It's not all that different now.

THE DAY THE CRIMINALS CAVED

One of my favorite stories about responsibly armed Americans is actually pretty funny. There was a police strike in a major Midwestern city—it may have been St. Louis, but that's not important. (I'd also like to point out right off the bat that this is NOT an anti-law enforcement story. They're the good guys.)

So the police union decided to go on strike one weekend and they predicted that there would be a crime wave without their presence on the street. Their intent was to show how valuable their services were in keeping the city safe.

But they were wrong. Absolutely no crime went down at all!

Why? Because without the police officers on patrol, the only people out there who were armed other than the criminals were citizens. Criminals aren't stupid—well, they are, but they're not stupid about things like this. They know citizens don't have protocols to follow like police officers do. They don't have extensive training on how to deal with armed assailants or have to follow certain steps or have chiefs to answer to if something isn't done exactly right.

Responsibly armed citizens are smart people. They don't arm themselves on a whim. I don't care how much ju jitsu Grandma has done—that's not going to stop a 6'6", 250-pound thug when he breaks into her house. That's why grandmas buy themselves guns, particularly if they live in an area where crime is a problem.

Those criminals knew that they ran the risk of encountering a very angry grandma pointing a gun at them. That grandma doesn't care about those criminals at all. What does she care about? Her house and her safety. (And when she hears that there are no cops patrolling her neighborhood, which isn't like it used to be when she moved in forty years ago...well, that can really tick a grandma off.) She's reached the point where she's going to take matters into her own hands if she has to, since there's nobody between her and the person who thinks her house is an easy target. She's now speaking a common language with a thug who tries breaking in—she's going to put a hole in his body somewhere. Pretty clear, huh?

As it turned out, the strike didn't last very long. I think the police union realized it was a bad idea and that the crime-free weekend didn't do anything for their cause.

I personally don't think many Americans study the past, at least not beyond what we are required to learn in school. People are more concerned about what's on television or what the government perspective is on things. You know what? I think we actually get the government we deserve. *We* are the people who elected that government. We do our Founding Fathers a disservice when we don't take an active role in learning and understanding who and what we are voting into office.

That lesson really applies to anything in life. I attribute my great successes and my miserable failures to my freedom, because whatever I do, I really am the person responsible for the outcomes. Even telling my story wouldn't be possible without natural-born freedom.

Now, the tradeoff is that this freedom comes with responsibility. It would be irresponsible to yell "fire" in a crowded theater or to drive 100 mph through a school zone on a school day. We have the freedom to skip paying our taxes on April 15, but that's not a good idea either. The issue really boils down to the fact that our actions cannot impede or harm others' freedom and rights either. Freedom comes with an inherent degree of responsibility. That's the social contract part of it. You can't just go out and do whatever you so choose in the name of personal freedom. It doesn't work that way and it shouldn't work that way.

I credit my parents for my ability to perceive and understand my personal freedom. I didn't have a single epiphany that brought me to it, but rather realized the power of freedom and what it could do for my life in phases. I think freedom is a do-it-yourself-kit for people—it takes purposeful intention to make it work in your life. Freedom is an inalienable right each of us shares, but there is a gap between possessing something and making it work. I may own a boat, but it could sit in my driveway because I haven't learned how to take it down to the lake and captain it. It takes intention, education, and practice to do anything. That's when the training wheels come off in life, when you grab something—an activity, an idea, anything—and just do it.

Freedom is not free. It's a cliché for sure, but it is true. One of the biggest cancers on American society is that people think freedom is about things given to them: you can get more than enough food with basic welfare benefits, along with a free basic cell phone. A family can get a big screen television and a couch to lie on all day without too much effort, and that becomes the place to sit all day without the need to do much else. Food, power, rent, even health care...it is really provided to those who want to take it. But that's not freedom—nor is it a way to go through life.

Freedom requires work—your work and my work. It's *our* responsibility. If you don't do your work, who do you expect will do it for you? That's basically the crux of my dad's mantra: "If it is to be, it's up to me." There is freedom in being able to do that.

But let's shift this a little from focusing on our individual freedom to the responsibility we have to our families. My family is one of the most precious things I have. They bring me so much love—and so much joy—that it is almost impossible to put into words. Because my family is so precious to me, I have a burning desire to protect them, and I have the freedom, as affirmed by the Second Amendment, to do that. Isn't that terrific?

We all have the responsibility for protecting our mutual and individual freedoms, but we must be vigilant. We all have a serious responsibility to preserve freedom's potency—and it's a heck of a powerful thing, particularly when it's absent—because it can atrophy. When that happens, we not only lose our freedom, but our rights and our dreams. It's something that's difficult to get back and re-establish once it's gone, too.

The natural right to defend yourself from unprovoked attack has been acknowledged and accepted since antiquity. I can't think of anyone who would argue that—even before primitive man could read and write and codify laws, it was happening. Nobody needed to write that down to make it a law. As we have the natural right to pursue life, liberty, and happiness, you would think it would be an absurd argument to assert these rights but have no means to prevent someone from taking them from us. How or why would someone think they have that right? And yet they do! That's just crazy.

The interesting thing is that throughout history, we've seen a serious focus on the importance of being able to defend ourselves. From Hammurabi's Code to Roman law to St. Thomas Aquinas, there's just no question that the practice of self-defense has always been viewed as a natural-born freedom. And why have humans spent so much time trying to safeguard this freedom? Because despite it being God-given, there's an inherent risk of our fellow man—even our own government—trying to take it away. Check this out:

> *"If the theft has been done by night, if the owner kills the thief, the thief shall be held to lawfully killed." [Using deadly force against a thief; one may lawfully kill a thief who skulks in the night.]*

That's Roman law. Guess when it was written? Almost *2,500* years ago.

In the second edition of the *Catechism of the Catholic Church*, St. Thomas Aquinas wrote:

> *2263 The legitimate defense of persons and societies is not an exception to the prohibition against the murder of the innocent that constitutes intentional killing. "The act of self-defense can have a double effect: the preservation*

of one's own life; and the killing of the aggressor...The one is intended, the other is not."

2264 Love toward one's self remains a fundamental principle of morality. Therefore it is legitimate to insist on respect for one's own right to life. Someone who defends his life is not guilty of murder even if he is forced to deal his aggressor a lethal blow: "If a man in self-defense uses more than necessary violence, it will be unlawful: whereas if he repeals force with moderation, his defense will be lawful...Nor is killing for salvation that a man omit the act of moderate self-defense to avoid killing the other man, since one is bound to take more care of one's own life than of the others."

So now we have St. Thomas Aquinas weighing in on this too. You don't have to be a Catholic to appreciate his thoughts either—as a man, he was known as a philosopher who was particularly interested in natural law. He's considered the Catholic church's greatest theologian and philosopher and his work forms the core for any man considering the priesthood.

I like what Aquinas says because he views self-defense as a reasonable act, and I think most people who carry would agree with him. If you're put in a position where you're defending yourself and your family, you are going to do what is reasonable to protect yourself, and probably no more than that. Your only interest is to stop the threat—not to use excessive violence or actions in the process.

It's interesting because the anti-gunners are all about stopping violence, and assume gun owners are violent people. But that's so far from the truth. It is purely about defense for those who choose to carry. We don't go out there and incite violence. We go about our business and take care of protecting our own lives and the lives of those we love.

And remember John Locke, the philosopher I mentioned earlier in this chapter? He makes a simple proclamation in *The Second Treatise of Civil Government:*

> *I should have a right to destroy that which threatens me with destruction: for, by the fundamental law of nature, man being to be preserved as much as possible, when all cannot be preserved, the safety of the innocent is to be preferred; and one may destroy a man who makes war upon him, or has discovered an enmity to his being, for the same reason that he may kill a wolf or a lion; because such men are not under the ties of the common law of reason, have no other rule, but that of force and violence, and so may be treated as beasts of prey, those dangerous and noxious creatures, that will be sure to destroy him whenever he falls into their power.*

He makes a good point here, one that ties into the freedom to defend ourselves. Most likely, if we are put into the position of actively defending ourselves with our guns, it is against an unreasonable criminal, one who cares little about laws and even less about our lives. We have little need to defend ourselves against our neighbors and friends who abide by the law.

When I carry in public, most people around me don't know. There really is no need for them to know. It's for my protection. And God willing, I will never need to exert that freedom.

There is extensive writing and analysis regarding the self-defense facet of natural law, common law, and statute law. The concept that self-defense is an individual right, a freedom, is not some fabricated illusion; it is well-grounded and cannot be misconstrued. Amazingly, there are still many people out there who attempt to pervert the true intent.

THE USCCA AND THE SUPREME COURT RULING

I'm a huge fan of history, as you can probably tell. One of my proudest moments with the USCCA has to do with a monumental Second Amendment case that will certainly go down in history.

In 2009, the Supreme Court was debating a case, McDonald vs. Chicago, which dealt with Second Amendment rights. Until this point, the Second Amendment had only been applied to the federal government and not to individual states. This made it possible for individual states and municipalities to pass restrictive gun laws that disregarded our Constitutional rights.

The consensus of the gun industry was that we needed to get involved because the outcome could potentially be disastrous to individual freedom as it pertains to owning and using a firearm in self-defense.

What we did was partner with Buckeye Firearms Foundation to research a specific aspect of this case. Now really, anyone who wants to spend the money can do this, but we really felt this was important. So we hired a

Constitutional expert to research and write an Amicus brief (Amicus means "friend of the court" and it is filed by someone who is not part of the case), which was submitted to the court.

It's a pretty complex and particular process to do this. Beyond the research, you have to follow specific guidelines and some ridiculous requirements, like using one specific printer that the court always uses. I imagine they've probably been using this same printer since the court was established...that's how historic this process is.

Now, because this was a pretty high-profile case, a lot of briefs were submitted to the court for review. What was really cool, though, was that of all those briefs, only two were mentioned. Ours was one of them, and it was mentioned by Justice Anthony Scalia in his non-dissenting opinion. We're part of history now.

And to make it even better, our side did win the case. In June 2010, The Supreme Court agreed that the residents of Chicago were legally able to keep handguns in their homes.

Even though I strongly believe in the Second Amendment, I never expected that I would get so personally involved in it. In addition to the USCCA's work on the *McDonald vs. Chicago* brief, I also have had the unique experience of talking about the Second Amendment in front of thousands of people on—where else?—the Washington Mall.

I am a reluctant public speaker by nature, and while it has turned into a natural extension of my work with the USCCA, that reluctance never really goes away. It certainly was still there on April 19, 2010—Patriot's Day—in Washington, D.C. Patriot's Day commemorates the Battles of Lexington and Concord on April 19, 1775—which was the first day of our war for independence.

Two hundred and thirty five years later, I was having my own little battle. My knees were shaking, my throat was dry, and when I opened my mouth, my voice was shaky. But I was there on the Mall for the Second Amendment March. The USCCA was one of the event sponsors, and I had been invited to speak. This was not an opportunity I wanted to pass up.

I had to talk for about five or six minutes and I memorized the entire speech. I was nervous as heck and I knew if I didn't do that, I'd be in the weeds at some point. I didn't sleep the night before. It was a big corner to turn for the USCCA, too, as a sponsor.

The speech itself is on YouTube if you want to see it. It was your basic Second Amendment speech. I think I did okay. Well, I probably did better than okay. The 3,000 people out there on the Mall stayed and listened and seemed to respond well to it, and that's all you can really ask for when you are giving a speech like that.

What really struck me while I was giving that speech was just how far the USCCA had come. It was hard for me to believe that the USCCA had gone from being just an idea that had nearly bankrupted me to a national organization with tens of thousands of members in less than five years. All of us were dedicated to our Constitution, the Bill of Rights (specifically the Second Amendment), and being responsibly armed Americans.

My dad's words also echoed in my mind—"If it is to be, it's up to me"—and I remember thinking, well, now it is. And it was awesome. Truly awesome.

It was humbling that day to walk around before and after the speech to meet some of the Second Amendment March attendees. The crazy part was that a lot of those people knew who I was, and they treated me as if I was their brother or their son. It was heartwarming and gratifying to meet people who shared the same intense desire to protect their families as I did.

It also affirmed to me that there was much more work to be done. I came back infused with energy for the USCCA. The event had actually fueled the idea for the Self-Defense SHIELD, and I came home and got to work on it. It was an important concept that I just knew would further protect the freedom that comes with our Second Amendment rights.

You know, some argue that self-defense is not an individual right. They say it's a collective right, meaning society as a *whole* has a right to defend itself, but must rely on specially trained professionals (law enforcement) for that defense. In other words, *you* shouldn't have the right to protect yourself and your loved ones. Someone else needs to do that for you. I call BS on that. No offense to the police, but they simply can't be everywhere. Sometimes, all that stands between you and someone else is your gun.

The way I see it, the only other option besides self-defense is no defense, and, well, I refuse to entertain *that*.

SHERIFF DAVID CLARKE
SAID IT BEST

Like him or hate him, Milwaukee County Sheriff David Clarke, Jr. certainly is on a lot of people's radar. Frankly, I like him a lot. He's a good guy and he's a friend of the USCCA. In 2013, Sheriff Clarke released a 30-second public service announcement that upset some people. You can find it on You Tube if you want to hear it, but here's the transcript:

"I'm Sheriff David Clarke, and I want to talk to you about something personal: your safety. It's no longer a spectator sport. I need you in the game, but are you ready? With officers laid off and furloughed, simply calling 911 and waiting is no longer your best option.

You can beg for mercy from a violent criminal, hide under the bed, or you can fight back; but are you prepared? Consider taking a certified safety course in handling a firearm so you can defend yourself until we get there. You have a duty to protect yourself and your family. We're partners now. Can I count on you?"

You can't get much clearer than that, can you? We live in a country where we have the freedom to do exactly what David Clarke suggests. And some people, heck, they're too scared to take that responsibility into their own hands. Which is fine. It's not for everyone. There are some people out there who shouldn't accept it—I'm sure you can think of a few among those you know. But there are others who definitely should—

they're a special group of people that understands that evil exists and that is willing to stand up against it.

Do you want to know who the police are? They act as a mild deterrent, and beyond their presence in society, if you think about it, they're really just the guys who come and clean up the mess AFTER it happens.

I don't know about you, but I don't like the idea of waiting around for someone else to protect me or my family from harm. That's MY job.

As a member of the 13th generation of Americans since the founding of our country, I think we successive generations run into a problem of taking our freedom for granted. Sure, we're all required to study history in school, but too many people never revisit those ideas. We hear about politics and the media tells us what they think we want and need to hear. Familiarity breeds contempt. The good news is that the system our Founding Fathers set up really is simple. Freedom for dummies, in a way. It's easy to understand. If you can understand it in fourth grade, you can understand it as an adult.

There will always be people who fundamentally oppose freedom— even among those who consider themselves Americans. They react out of fear and of not wanting the responsibilities that come with freedom. I don't understand why these people choose this perspective. Maybe they don't want to make the effort. Maybe they've never experienced what life has to offer. But let me tell you: I know I'm lucky to be alive, and I'm going to do whatever I can to make sure I *stay* alive for a long time.

We are not a country that should ever accept what someone says is good for us—we already said "no thanks" to England once and we put up a fight to back that up. We are a country of free individuals who cannot and should not be coerced into doing things by fear or threat of force. If you look back at our history, that's something our Founding Fathers strongly believed in. It's something I believe in, too.

THE FUTURE

> *I joined the USCCA to give me the peace of*
> *mind to protect my family.*
>
> – Norman C., PA

At the time of this writing, Delta Defense and the USCCA are planning to break ground on a brand new headquarters in West Bend, Wisconsin. Phase one of this new building will be approximately 65,000 square feet. That's over twice the size of the two current offices we occupy. Does this make me nervous? Heck yeah, it does! But here's what I've come to discover: if you're not doing something that makes you uncomfortable, you're not pushing hard enough.

Now, don't get me wrong. By no means am I suggesting that people make poor or rash business decisions. I assure you, I've made hundreds of forecasts and spreadsheets to make the most informed decision I can possibly make regarding how much space this business will need. But at the end of the day, you have to trust your research and then trust your gut. That's what I LOVE about the game of business. It's all about information, discipline, and gut instinct.

When you combine a natural love of business with a business that you're passionate about, well…that's when magical things happen. There's absolutely nothing I'd rather be doing than figuring out new and better ways to provide value to people who are willing to take full responsibility for the safety and protection of their families and loved ones. I consider it a blessing and an honor to be in the position that I'm in.

A question I hear a lot from fellow USCCA members is, "Tim, what is the future of concealed carry in the United States?" The answers to this question give me hope. You see, I have the opportunity to communicate with hundreds—if not thousands—of responsibly armed Americans on a regular basis. What I hear and see from this is encouraging. Every day, I see more and more Americans coming to the realization that it IS their responsibility to be that first line of defense for their families. Not only are they making this realization, but they're also taking the appropriate steps to become properly educated, trained, and insured.

No, I DON'T see a future America that looks like the old "Wild West," where everyone has a six-shooter strapped to their hip. Rather, I see a future where a large percentage of Americans will have taken up the "responsibly armed" lifestyle. They will discreetly carry concealed. They will be well trained, prepared, and ready to act on a moment's notice. And THIS new paradigm will usher in a brand new era of FEAR. However, the people experiencing this fear will be the criminals, the terrorists, and the evildoers. This new fear will make the lives of our police officers much safer and more enjoyable. Our communities will be safer. Our children will be safer. This vision of mine is in perfect harmony with my ultimate life mission:

My mission in life (and the mission of the USCCA) is to *Teach* 10 million people, *Insure* 1 million members, *Stop* 20,000 crimes, and *Save* 1,000 lives.

MY MISSION

Teach 10,000,000 people...
Insure 1,000,000 members...
Stop 20,000 crimes...
Save 1,000 lives!

We're well on our way to achieving this mission and I hope you will be a part of it.

The final message I have is for YOU, the responsibly armed American. I admire and respect you. I can relate 100% with the way you think and with what you believe. You are the sheepdog surrounded by a society of mostly sheep. You do not run away from trouble when your family is being threatened. You run toward it.

You are the glue that keeps our society together. You are the deterrent that makes criminals pause and wonder, "Do I really want to attack that person?" You are willing to gladly accept the immense responsibility of being your family's first line of defense.

This may sound weird, but I truly love you for that. **I do.** And that's why I will always have your back.